THE GOD OF THE PHILOSOPHERS

THE GOD OF
THE PHILOSOPHERS

by

ANTHONY KENNY

CLARENDON PRESS · OXFORD

Oxford University Press, Walton Street, Oxford OX2 6DP

Oxford New York Toronto
Delhi Bombay Calcutta Madras Karachi
Petaling Jaya Singapore Hong Kong Tokyo
Nairobi Dar es Salaam Cape Town
Melbourne Auckland

and associated companies in
Beirut Berlin Ibadan Nicosia

Oxford is a trade mark of Oxford University Press

Published in the United States
by Oxford University Press, New York

British Library Cataloguing in Publication Data

Kenny, Anthony John Patrick
The God of the philosophers.
1. God—Attributes
I. Title
212   BT130   79–40157
ISBN 0–19–824594–7
ISBN 0–19–824968–3 (Pbk.)

Printed in Great Britain by
Billing & Sons Limited, Guildford,
London and Worcester

PREFACE

From 1970 to 1972 I held the Wilde Lecturership in Natural Religion in the University of Oxford. For the general topic of my lectures I chose the attributes of God: in 1970 I lectured on omniscience, in 1971 on omnipotence, and in 1972 on benevolence. Later I had the opportunity to give modified and abbreviated versions of the same course of lectures at Princeton, at Cornell, and at Calvin College, Grand Rapids. The present volume contains a version of the lectures that has been rewritten to take account of the discussions of those earlier courses and of some of the material that others have published in the intervening years. In the process of revision I have omitted much of the material from the original lectures: in particular I found that it was impossible to treat of divine benevolence without becoming too deeply involved in matters that are the province of the historian of dogma rather than of the philosopher of religion.

I am grateful to the Universities of Oxford, Princeton, and Cornell for inviting me to give these lectures, and to all those who took part in the discussions on the occasion of their delivery: in particular I am grateful to Peter Geach, Alvin Plantinga, and Terence Penelhum who were my fellow-lecturers at Calvin College during the very happy and fruitful summer institute where they were presented.

Part of Chapter II was presented at an American Philosophical Association symposium and was published in the Journal of Philosophy in 1971.

2 August 1978   ANTHONY KENNY

CONTENTS

Introduction

I.   *The God of the Philosophers*   3

Part One: Omniscience

II.   *The Eternal Truths*   15
III.   *Omniscience and Experience*   27
IV.   *Omniscience, Eternity, and Time*   38

Part Two: Foreknowledge

V.   *Foreknowledge and Indeterminism*   51
VI.   *Foreknowledge and Determinism*   72

Part Three: Omnipotence

VII.   *The Definition of Omnipotence*   91
VIII.   *Omnipotence and Time*   100
IX.   *Omnipotence and Goodness*   110

Conclusion

X.   *The God of Reason and the God of Faith*   121

Bibliography   130

Index   133

INTRODUCTION

I. THE GOD OF THE PHILOSOPHERS

This book is a study of some of the attributes traditionally ascribed to God in western theism. The aim of the study is a philosophical one rather than a theological one: it is to discuss the concept of God and his attributes in the light of reason without accepting as authoritative any claim to revelation, such as the Christian revelation. The study will be an exercise in the traditional discipline of natural theology—a discipline which was a philosophical, not a theological, one.

Though commonly undertaken by believers, the practice of natural theology by itself does not commit one either to belief or disbelief in the existence of God. As the atheist philosopher Antony Flew has pointed out (1955, 10), in the *Dialogues concerning Natural Religion* David Hume is clearly practising the same discipline as St. Thomas Aquinas in the *Summa contra Gentiles*. The inquiry is a conceptual one concerning the coherence of a group of attributes. Is it logically possible for there to be an entity possessing the traditional attributes of God?

The word 'natural' in the expression 'natural theology' is meant to mark a contrast between nature and revelation. Natural theology is not natural in the sense of being a simple and unsophisticated activity: the concept of natural religion is the product of a fairly sophisticated state of western theism and would have been foreign to many great religious thinkers before the Middle Ages. The concept emerged in an age in which theologians, reflecting on what they believed, made a distinction between those elements which they thought could be established by unaided reason and those parts they thought due to the supernatural revelation of God in the Bible, through Moses and Christ, and in the history of the Jewish faith and the Christian church.

The possibility of natural theology has been denied by some theologians and by some philosophers. The theological arguments against natural theology are mostly concerned with the relationship between reason and faith: they urge the uselessness of reason as a means to salvation and of philosophical speculation as a step on the road to heaven. The philosophical arguments against natural theology are often based on theories of meaning which would rule out as meaningless statements purporting to refer to any unobservable, transcendent entity such as the God of traditional theism. Both sets of objections attack not the possibility of natural theology as such, but the possibility of a positive and fruitful natural theology. For if we take natural theology to be the philosophical analysis of the concepts used in thinking and talking about God, then a disproof of God's existence, or a demonstration that the very notion of God was incoherent, would itself be a sucessful piece of natural theologizing.

In the final chapter I shall say something about the relationship between philosophical speculation about the divine attributes and religious faith in a saving God. The question whether statements about divine attributes are meaningful and coherent is, in a manner, the topic of the whole book: but it will be well to say something immediately about the particular way in which the challenge to a constructive natural theology presents itself in certain philosophical quarters.

'What difference in experience', those influenced by logical positivism sometimes ask, 'does it make if God exists, or would it make if God did not exist?' 'What is the difference', we may be asked, 'between the world being as it is, and there being a God, and the world being as it is, and there being no God?' Theists have been embarrassed by the question, and have struggled to find an answer.

Trying to answer this question is a game one cannot win; but that shows nothing about the meaningfulness of religious language. For given any proposition p, and asked 'What is the difference between the world's being as it is, and p, and on the other hand the world's being as it is, and not p?', one cannot give any answer. If one answers: 'The difference is that in the one case p, and in the other case not p', then one's answer is dismissed as uninformative. The same happens if one offers as an answer any proposition q synonymous with p. On the other hand, if one brings in some other proposition q which is not synonymous with p, and says that the difference is q, then since q is not synonymous with p, one will be asked: 'Well, what is the difference between q plus p's being the case, and q plus p's not being the case?' and the game will recommence.

This tactic is available no matter what p may be (as critics of the positivist approach have shown by taking as a substitution for 'p' the proposition that other minds exist) and so if it is effective in showing that religious language is meaningless, it is available to show that any language whatever is meaningless.

It is in any case erroneous to take whole sentences as units of meaning and inquire about their meaningfulness or meaninglessness. Sentences are composite, articulate, and their meaning and meaningfulness is a function of the expressions they contain. Of course a sentence may be built up out of meaningful expressions without itself being meaningful; but even the meaninglessness of sentences is a function of the expressions they contain. We know that 'colourless green ideas sleep furiously' is meaningless because we know the meaning of the expressions it contains, not because of any researches into the verifiability or falsifiability of the sentence as a whole.

For this reason anyone who is interested in the question of the existence of God has to study first of all the divine attributes; for to say that God exists is to say that there is something that has the divine attributes; and if 'God exists' is to be true, then the divine attributes must at least themselves be coherent and jointly compatible. The coherence of the notion of God, as possessor of the traditional divine attributes, is a necessary, though of course not sufficient, condition for God's existence.

I shall single out for discussion two of the traditional attributes of God: omniscience and omnipotence. Both these attributes are ascribed to God by the great majority of Christian, Jewish, and Muslim theologians. Other attributes, such as justice, mercy, and love, have a more obvious significance for the religious believer; but they are also less immediately amenable to philosophical investigation and analysis. In the first place, some theologians would say that only revelation and not unaided reason can give us grounds for thinking that predicates such as 'just', 'merciful', and 'loving' can be applied to God; in the second place, whatever significance these predicates have when applied to God, they cannot be understood simply in the same sense as when applied to human beings. Intellect and power, on the other hand, are intended to be attributed to God in the most literal sense: it is the infinity of the intellect and the limitlessness of the power that makes the difference between the creator and the creature. 'Omniscient' and 'omnipotent' are not predicates which were in use for application to human beings and are then ascribed in some transferred or analogical sense to God: they express concepts which were devised to represent uniquely divine characteristics. Each concept is the result of reflection by philosophers or philosophically minded theologians upon elements in the religious tradition of western theism.

Homer, long ago, stated that the gods knew everything (*Odyssey*, IV, 379). But it is clear that this is not to be taken literally: much in the *Iliad* goes on behind the back of Zeus, and the plot of the *Odyssey* can only start because of the inadvertence of Poseidon. Xenophon reported that it was a peculiarity of Socrates to believe that the gods knew literally everything, all that was said and done and even things only planned in silence. Plato, in the *Laws* (884c. ff.), provided the death penalty not only for those who denied the existence of God, but for those who while confessing that the gods existed denied that they took any notice of the affairs of men. In the Old Testament, God knows the future, whether hidden in natural causes or dependent on the intentions and plans of human beings: the Book of Job hymns the divine knowledge of all the mysteries of nature, and Psalm 139 tells how men's most secret thoughts have nowhere to hide from the all-seeing eye of God. According to the writer of Isaiah it is Yahweh's knowledge of the future which marks him as the true God in contrast to the sham gods of the heathen. The Old Testament teaching is echoed by Jesus (Matt. 11: 21) and by the author of the Epistle to the Hebrews (Heb. 4:13).

The Old and New Testament passages describing God's knowledge are too poetical and rhetorical for it to be possible to decide how literally their writers intended the idea that God knows everything. Several Stoic thinkers seem to have believed that some things were too insignificant for God to know and that there were details that it would be beneath God's dignity to concern himself with. This tradition is echoed among the Church Fathers by St. Jerome, who at one point says that it is absurd to suggest that God knows at every moment how many gnats are born or die, how many fleas there are in the world, and how many fish in the sea. Later theological writers were embarrassed by such texts and insisted that God was quite literally omniscient.

From the time of Origen and Augustine theologians have reflected on the problems which arise for other religious doctrines if God is conceived to know everything. What is the point of prayer if God already knows all our needs and desires? How can human actions be free if God already knows what they will be before the thought of performing them has even entered into their agents' heads? This latter problem was clearly set out by Boethius in the sixth century. 'If God beholds all things and God cannot be deceived, that must of necessity follow which His providence foresees as to come. Wherefore, if from eternity He foreknows not only the deeds of men but also their counsels and wills there can be no free will.'[1] Boethius's answer to the problem was that God's foreknowledge was not really foreknowledge: because God's eternal life was simultaneous with the whole of history, God's knowledge was not knowledge in advance. From a human point of view a particular action might be future: it was not so from the divine viewpoint; and so actions which to us are future are not determined by the eternity of God's vision of them.

Medieval scholastics such as Thomas Aquinas, Duns Scotus, and William Ockham elaborated theories of omniscience and foreknowledge against the background of the writings of Augustine and Boethius. They connected the problems with Aristotle's treatment of the logic of future contingent propositions in the *De Interpretatione*. The discussion developed, in the fifteenth century, into an adumbration of a three-valued logic. No agreement was reached in the Middle Ages about the appropriate way to reconcile divine foreknowledge of the future with the freedom of human action.

All medieval Catholic writers, however, agreed both that God has infallible and fully detailed knowledge of the future, and that human actions are free and undetermined. At the Reformation Protestant writers were found to deny both of these doctrines, so that the debate became broader and more complicated. Within both the Catholic and the Protestant camp controversies developed between those who emphasized divine knowledge and power at the expense of human freedom, and those who insisted on the indeterminacy of human action in a way difficult to reconcile with God's knowledge of the future. The most elaborate attempt at a

---

[1] 'Si cuncta prospicit Deus neque falli ullo modo potest, evenire necesse est, quod providentia futurum esse praeviderit. Quare si ab aeterno non facta hominum modo, sed etiam consilia voluntatesque praenoscit, nulla erit arbitrii libertas' (*De Consolatione Philosophiae*, V. pr. 3).

libertarian solution to Boethius's problem was the theory of *scientia media* or middle knowledge devised by sixteenth-century Jesuits and later adopted among the reformed churches by Arminian theologians. The most forthright and capable statement of a determinist attempt to reconcile divine foreknowledge and human responsibility was in the treatise on Freedom of the Will by the eighteenth-century Calvinist Jonathan Edwards. Nineteenth- and twentieth-century treatments of these matters have added very little to the work of earlier philosophers and theologians.

The theological doctrine of omnipotence, like that of omniscience, is based on biblical and Greek material. One of the names of God in the Old Testament is El Shadday, which was translated *pantokrator* in the Greek Septuagint and *omnipotens* in the Latin vulgate. God's gigantic power is seen both in the history of Israel and in the government of heaven and earth: Job, after listening to Yahweh's recital of the wonders of creation confesses 'I know that you are all-powerful: what you can conceive you can perform' (Job 42:2). Jesus, having astonished his disciples by saying that it was easier for a camel to pass through the eye of a needle than for a rich man to enter the kingdom of heaven, so that they asked 'Who then can be saved?', comforted them by saying 'With God everything is possible' (Matt. 19:25–6).

Among Greek writers Agathon, Xenophon, and Callimachus can be cited as expressing belief in divine omnipotence.[1] But difficulties in the doctrine were also much aired in classical antiquity: Lucretius produces a number of problems (5, 86–90), and Pliny, in his *Natural History* (2, 27), lists a number of things impossible to deity: to commit suicide, to alter the past, to revoke mathematical truths. In late antiquity it was a frequent topic of debate whether the gods were ruled by fate or not.

The Christian creeds begin with an expression of faith in God as almighty: the Greek and Latin words involved connote divine sovereignty over all things rather than ability to do everything. Omnipotence no doubt involves universal lordship, but the converse is not necessarily true: complete control over all creatures does not necessarily imply the ability to perform every conceivable feat.

Omnipotence, like omniscience, was a topic of study and debate in medieval scholasticism. At the beginning of the Middle Ages

---

[1] The texts are conveniently collected in Pease, 1955, 668.

Berengar of Tours argued for a strictly limited conception of divine omnipotence (see Hunt, 1943, 226), while Peter Damiani understood the doctrine in such a broad sense that he is often taken to have taught that God could cancel the past. (See, for instance, Damiani, 1943, 70.)

Peter Abelard was condemned at the Council of Sens (1140) for saying that God could not do otherwise than he had done (Denzinger, 374). Being bound by his goodness to do whatever was best, Abelard had argued, God could have acted otherwise only in the sense that if—*per impossibile*—he had wished to do so nothing would have prevented him from doing so. Aquinas thought that this put too great limits on God's power: no doubt God could not have made the present world better than he has, but he could have made other, better worlds. But Aquinas agreed with Abelard that God was incapable of sinning or doing anything wicked. (*S.Th.* Ia, 25, 5–6).

Later in the Middle Ages, however, Ockham seems to have taught that God could in a certain sense make wrong into right, and could command men to hate himself (Copleston, 1953, 105). Wycliff went so far as to say that God actually willed men to sin, and willed the acts of will by which they sin: feats which Abelard and Aquinas would have regarded as impossible to God. But on the other hand Wycliff limited God's omnipotence by asserting that even on the broadest interpretation of divine power God could not create a better world than the one which he in fact created. He was condemned, at the Council of Constance, for saying that everything that happened, happened of necessity (Denzinger, 1952, 607; see Robson, 1961, 230).

After the Renaissance the positions of Descartes, Leibniz, and Spinoza can be contrasted in the same way as those of Ockham, Abelard, and Wycliff. Descartes, like Ockham, set no limits to divine power: God can do, according to him, even what seems logically impossible to us. (See Chapter II below.) Leibniz, like Abelard, thought that of a number of absolutely possible worlds, God could make only the best, being obliged thereto by his wisdom (*Theodicy*, I, 8). Spinoza, like Wycliff, thought that only the actual world is possible, and everything that happens happens by necessity, by divine necessity (*Ethics*, I, 33).

In discussing omniscience and omnipotence in the present work I shall not follow the historical order in which the doctrines were developed, controverted, and modified. I shall consider the topics in an order suggested by logical and philosophical rather than historical considerations.

The first of the three parts into which the book is divided will concern omniscience in general. The doctrine of omniscience is easy to formulate precisely: it is the doctrine that for all p, if p, then God knows that p. We may study the various facets of the doctrine by considering in turn different types of substitution for 'p' in this formulation of the doctrine. In Chapter II I shall consider God's knowledge of the truths of logic and mathematics: the case in which what is substituted for 'p' is a necessary proposition. In Chapter III I shall consider the case in which what is substituted is an empirical proposition: I shall treat of God's knowledge of matters of experience. In Chapter IV I shall consider problems about divine knowledge of time: the problems which arise when one attends to the tense of propositions substituted for 'p' in the definition of omniscience.

The second part of the book concerns a particular aspect of omniscience which both historically and doctrinally is the most important aspect: divine foreknowledge of contingent future matters such as free human actions. It is divided into two sections, the first of which treats the problems as they are seen from an indeterminist standpoint, and the second of which considers the solutions proposed against a determinist background. The first of these sections, Chapter V, will involve a consideration of substitutions for 'p' in 'for all p, if p, then God knows that p' involving counterfactual conditionals.

The third main part of the book is devoted to omnipotence. This doctrine is not capable of simple and uncontroversial formulation as is the doctrine of omniscience: accordingly, the first chapter of this part, Chapter VII, is devoted to the search for a satisfactory definition of omnipotence. Chapter VIII is concerned with the most interesting of the problems which arise about divine omnipotence: the question whether God can change, or cancel, or bring about the past.

The conclusion that emerges from the three main sections of the book is that the traditional doctrines of omniscience and omnipotence cannot be stated in a way which makes them compatible with other traditional doctrines such as that of divine immutability, divine lack of responsibility for sin, and human freedom of

the will. The final chapter of the book inquires into the consequences of this philosophical conclusion for the rationality of
religious belief in God.

PART ONE

OMNISCIENCE

II. THE ETERNAL TRUTHS

If God knows everything, then among the truths that he knows are the *a priori* truths of logic and mathematics. If God knows everything, then he knows that contradictories cannot be true together; he knows that $2+2=4$ and that the three angles of a Euclidean triangle add up to two right angles. These, after all, are truths which we know. So any omniscient being must know them to be true.

Not surprisingly, the Bible has nothing to say about divine knowledge of *a priori* truth. It seems to have been the impact of Platonism on Christianity which led to connections being drawn between God and mathematics. St. Augustine in his book *On Free Will* (2, 12 ff.) presents an argument for the existence of God which is based on the eternity of truth. He says: 'There are things I touch with my bodily senses, like the sky and the earth and all I see them to contain. I do not know how long any of these things are going to last. But 7 and 3 make 10 not only now but for ever; there never was a time when 7 and 3 did not make 10 and there never will be a time when they do not make 10.' Knowledge of numbers and their relations, Augustine argues, cannot have come from our senses. The objects of mathematics are not inferior to us in the way that bodies are:

Bodies are things about which we make judgements: we say that this is not as white as it should be, or not square enough, and so on . . . We judge such things according to those inner rules of truth that we discern in common, but no one judges in any way of the rules themselves . . . When anyone says that . . . 7 and 3 are 10, no one says that it should have been the case; knowing that it is the case, men do not criticise it like examiners but rejoice in it like discoverers.

The truths of mathematics cannot be on the same level as our minds, because if they were they would be no less changeable than our minds are. Therefore they are something higher than our minds. Imagining an adversary who is prepared to admit that if there is anything higher than our minds it is God, Augustine claims to have proved that God exists. For if there is something more excellent again than truth, then that is God; but if not, then truth itself is God. 'Whether therefore there is thus a more excellent thing, or whether there is not, you cannot deny that God exists.'

An essential step in Augustine's argument is the claim that mathematical truths are discovered and not invented by the mind. This is a typical expression of Platonism in mathematics. Of course 'Platonism' is an unhelpful word. 'Platonism' in philosophy, like 'Fascism' in politics, is a word whose evaluative meaning has eroded its descriptive meaning. 'Platonist', like 'Fascist', is a name people are more prepared to call others than to claim for their own. Still, Augustine was a Platonist in the straightforward sense that he accepted Plato's theory of ideas or forms. In his book, *Eighty-three Different Questions* (46, 1–2), he says: 'Ideas are the primary forms, or the permanent and immutable reasons of real things, and they are not themselves formed; so they are, as a consequence, eternal and ever the same in themselves and they are contained in the divine intelligence.' Augustine gives a theological turn to the Platonic theory: it is because the ideas are in the divine mind that they are eternal and immutable. When God created, he did not look to any paradigm outside himself.

In this Augustine differs from Plato and from modern Platonist mathematicians. For him, what ultimately gives truth to a truth of mathematics (for instance, the truth that the diameter of a circle is larger than any chord) is not something outside the mind, though it is outside any human mind. Contemporary Platonism, on the other hand, insists that mathematical truths are not truths about the contents of any mind.

Platonism in the modern sense is discussed very clearly in the writings of Descartes. In 1630, a decade before the completion of the *Meditations*, Descartes began working on what he called the metaphysical foundations of physics. In a letter to his friend, Father Mersenne, on 15 April 1630, he wrote as follows:

The mathematical truths which you call eternal have been laid down by God and depend on Him entirely no less than the rest of His creatures. Indeed, to say that these truths are independent of God is to talk of Him as if He were Jupiter or Saturn and to subject Him to the Styx and the Fates. Please do not hesitate to assert and proclaim everywhere that it is God who has laid down these laws in nature just as a king lays down laws in his kingdom. There is no single one that we cannot understand if our mind turns to consider it . . . It will be said that if

God had established these truths He could change them as a king changes his laws. To this the answer is: 'Yes he can, if His will can change.' 'But I understand them to be eternal and unchangeable.'—'I make the same judgment about God.' 'But His will is free.'—'Yes, but His power is incomprehensible.' (AT I, 135; K, 11)

In this letter Descartes writes as if it was 'an almost universal way of imagining God' to treat mathematical truths as independent of him. This was not in fact correct. In scholastic thought mathematical essences were independent of God's will, but were entirely dependent on God's essence.[1] Aquinas, for instance, discussing the nature of God's knowledge of the essences of creatures, says that, since the essence of God contains all that makes for perfection in the essence of every other thing, and more beside, God can know all things in his own essence, with a knowledge of what is proper to each (*S.Th.* Ia, 14, 5–6).

Mersenne himself, however, seems to have been prepared to defend the view that the mathematical truths were altogether independent of God; and in his next letter Descartes returned to the attack.

As for the eternal truths, I say once more that they are true or possible only because God knows them as true or possible. They are not known as true by God in any way which would imply that they are true independently of Him . . . In God willing and knowing are a single thing, in such a way that by the very fact of willing something He knows it, and it is only for this reason that such a thing is true. (AT I, 147; K, 13)

Why does Descartes say that the mathematical truths are 'true or possible' (*verae aut possibiles*)? Surely mathematical truths are necessary truths? One way of interpreting this would be to say: the eternal truths are true if there are material objects to be models for them; otherwise they are merely possible. But since Descartes believed that in fact there are no material objects corresponding to the geometer's figures, actual bodies being too irregular (AT VII, 381; HR II, 227), and yet continues to speak of mathematical truths, which are true of these non-existent objects (AT VII, 116–18; HR II, 20–1), the most consistent way to take the expres-

---

[1] The scholastics preferred speaking of 'the essence of things' to using the Augustinian expression 'the eternal truths'; so much so that a writer like Scotus, discussing a passage where Augustine speaks of 'the incorporeal and eternal concept of a square', substitutes 'the essence of stone'. (Scotus, XVI, 281ff.).

sion is as meaning 'necessarily true of actual or possible objects'.

Descartes's third letter to Mersenne on the topic begins:

You ask me by what kind of causality God established the eternal truths. I reply: by the same kind of causality as he created all things, that is to say, as their efficient and total cause. For it is certain that he is no less the author of creatures' essence than he is of their existence; and this essence is nothing other than the eternal truths . . . I know that God is the author of everything and that these truths are something and consequently that he is their author. . . . You ask also what necessitated God to create these truths; and I reply that just as He was free not to create the world, so He was no less free to make it untrue that all the lines drawn from the centre of a circle to its circumference are equal. (AT I, 151; K, 14)

After this letter we hear no more of the eternal truths until the *Replies to the Fifth Objections*. Gassendi had objected to the talk in the *Fifth Meditation* of 'the immutable and eternal nature of a triangle'. It seems hard, he said, to set up any immutable and eternal nature in addition to God. Descartes replied:

It would seem rightly so if the question was about something which exists or if I was setting up something immutable whose immutability did not depend on God. . . . I do not think that the essences of things and the mathematical truths which can be known of them are independent of God, but I think that they are immutable and eternal because God so willed and so disposed. (AT VII, 380; HR II, 226)

The *Sixth Objections* took exception to Descartes's doctrine. The hand of Mersenne can be seen in the *Objections*, which repeat the language and queries of his letters of 1630 (AT VII, 417; HR II, 237). Descartes's reply covers familiar ground; but a letter to Mesland of 1644 adds some new points, including the following:

it was free and indifferent for God to make it not be true that the three angles of a triangle were equal to two right angles, or in general that contradictories could not be true together. . . . Even if God has willed that some truths should be necessary, this does not mean that he willed them necessarily; for it is one thing to will that they be necessary, and quite another to will them necessarily or to be necessitated to will them. (AT IV, 110; K, 151)

There are two ways in which Descartes's doctrine differs from that of traditional scholasticism. The first is its Platonic aspect: the mathematical essences are distinct from the essence of God. The second is its voluntarist aspect: the mathematical essences are under the control of God's will.

Voluntarism in mathematics is rejected explicitly by Aquinas in chapter 25 of the second book of *Summa contra Gentiles*:

Since the principles of some sciences, such as logic, geometry, and arithmetic, are drawn solely from the formal principles which constitute the essences of things, it follows that God cannot do anything which conflicts with these principles: thus, he cannot make a genus not predicable of its species, or bring it about that the radii of a circle are not equal, or that a rectilinear triangle should not have its three angles equal to two right angles.

In God, Descartes says, willing and knowing are a single thing; by the very fact of willing something he knows it. The doctrine of the simplicity of God—the doctrine that God has no parts—was common among scholastics: they would have agreed that in God intellect and will are a single thing. The will of God, the mind of God, the essence of God: these, they would have said, are all one and the same reality. They did not, however, understand this difficult doctrine as implying that whatever God knows he wills; nor did it prevent them from making distinctions between different types of knowledge and different types of will in God. For instance, they distinguished between God's knowledge of essences (which included actual and possible things) and his awareness of reality or *scientia visionis* (which concerned only what was actual). They distinguished also between two sorts of divine will; the will of permission, or consequent will (by which God willed whatever happened since it was always in his power to prevent it), and the will of good pleasure or antecedent will (by which he willed certain things, such as the salvation of the faithful, as values in themselves). If any coherent account can be given at all of the knowledge and will of God distinctions similar to those made by the scholastics have at some point to be drawn; and certainly Descartes himself elsewhere frequently drew them, as we shall later have occasion to see.

Descartes's Platonism is no less unorthodox than his voluntarism. Platonism about essences is discussed in detail by Duns Scotus in his commentary on the thirty-sixth distinction of Peter Lombard's *Sentences* (Scotus, XVII, 445 ff.). There are certain people, Scotus says, who divide things into three classes: (1) fictional beings, (2)

real beings without existence, or existential being (*esse existentiae*),
(3) real beings with existence. Even without existence, a real being
differs from a fictional being, in that it *can* have existence, and
therefore it has a certain absolute reality before it exists. This
absolute reality is called *esse essentiae*: it reminds a modern reader
of the status of Meinong's pure objects, beyond being and non-
being. This belongs to it because of its relationship to an exemplar
in the divine mind: just as God is the efficient cause of the existential
being of things, so he is the exemplar cause of their essential being.

The view here discussed clearly has similarities with that of
Descartes. Like Descartes's mathematical entities, the things with
essential being are distinct from God, since they stand in a causal
relationship to him. However, the relation is viewed as one of
exemplar causality, whereas Descartes viewed it as one of efficient
causality. 'God can be called the efficient cause (of the eternal
truths)' he said in the *Sixth Replies*, 'in the same way as the King
is the maker of the law, even though the law is not a physically
existent thing'. (AT VII, 436; HR II, 251.)

This Platonism is sharply criticized by Scotus. On this view, he
says, creation would not be creation *ex nihilo*. Something that has
essential being is, according to the theory, not nothing, and creation
would merely be the giving of existential being to what already
has essential being. The only activity of God that would really
count as creation *ex nihilo* would be the production of creatures in
their essential being; but this, according to the theory, is eternal,
and so creation would be *ab aeterno*. On Scotus's own view,
creatures are the objects of God's ideas not according to existential
being or essential being, but only according to an *esse diminutum*
which corresponds to what a modern writer might call 'intentional'
existence.

Scotus's criticism could be applied to Descartes. Though he
denied to Gassendi that he was setting up anything eternal
independent of God, he could not have denied that he was setting
up something eternal *distinct* from God: this is why he can be
called the father of modern Platonism. For ever since Augustine
had identified the Platonic ideas with archetypes in the divine
mind, no orthodox scholastic had ever admitted the existence of
anything eternal except God and God alone. But for Descartes
the geometers' triangle is an eternal creature of God, with its own
immutable nature and properties, a real thing lacking only the

perfection of actual existence. (AT VII, 64; HR I, 121. AT VII, 116–18; HR II, 19–21. AT VII, 383; HR II, 228.)

The eternal truths, then, do not depend on the human intellect, or on any existing things, but only on God who instituted them from eternity as a supreme legislator. When Descartes speaks of laws of mathematics—or, for that matter, of physics such as the law of inertia—the word 'law' has not, as it has for us, lost all connection with a legislator. And this perhaps gives us something of a clue as to why he differed from the scholastic theologians on the status of eternal truths. It was in order to provide a foundation for his physics.

The prime novelty in Descartes's physical system was the rejection of the Aristotelian apparatus of real qualities and sub-stantial forms: the first chapters of *Le Monde,* on which he was working at the material time, are a sustained polemic against these chimerical entities (AT XI, 3–36, and especially 37). Rejection of substantial forms entailed rejection of essences, since for Aristotelians the two are closely connected, essence being identical with form in the case of immaterial beings, and consisting of form plus the appropriate kind of matter in the case of material beings. Descartes did not reject the terminology of essence as firmly as he rejected that of form and quality, but he reinterpreted it drastically. When, in his letter to Mersenne of 27 May 1630 cited above, he says that the essences of creatures are nothing but the eternal truths, he is throwing over the idea that an essence might be a principle of explanation, an element in the constitution of a substance which might have causal effects on the history of the substance (as, e.g., the essence of an oak might be thought to provide an explanatory factor in the life-cycle of an oak).

Now in the Aristotelian system it was the forms and essences that provided the element of stability in the flux of phenomena which made it possible for there to be universally valid scientific knowledge. Having rejected essences and forms, Descartes needs a new foundation for the certain and immutable physics that he wishes to establish. If there are no substantial forms, what connects one moment of a thing's history to another?

The immutable will of God, replies Descartes, who has laid down the laws of nature, which are enshrined in the eternal truths (AT VII, 80; HR I, 192; AT XI, 37). These laws include not only the laws of logic and mathematics, but also the law of inertia and other laws of motion (AT III, 648; K, 136). Consequently they provide the foundations of mechanistic physics. The physics is immutable, because God's will is immutable.

But might not God have immutably willed that at a certain point in time the laws might change—just as Descartes wrote to Mesland that God contingently willed the laws to be necessary (AT IV, 110; K, 151)? If this possibility is to be ruled out, not only God's immutability but also God's veracity must be appealed to. God would be a deceiver if, while giving me such a nature that I perceive these laws as immutable, he had also decreed that the laws were to change. So the veracity of God is not only sufficient, but also necessary, to establish in Descartes's post-Aristotelian system the permanent validity of clearly and distinctly perceived truths.

It is time to turn from the historical to the philosophical consideration of the doctrine of eternal truths. Should a theist say, with Descartes, that the truths of mathematics are created by God? Or should he deny this, in company with mainstream scholasticism?

Questions about the possibility of God's knowledge often turn into questions about the nature of certain types of truth. In this present case too, a philosopher's views on the nature of divine knowledge of *a priori* truths will depend on his views about the nature of *a priori* truth itself. The nature of necessary truth has been much discussed in nineteenth- and twentieth-century philosophy of mathematics. Quine, in *From a Logical Point of View* (1953), has signalled a connection between contemporary debates on these topics and the medieval controversy about the nature of universals: 'The three main mediaeval points of view regarding universals are designated by historians as realism, conceptualism, and nominalism. Essentially the same three doctrines reappear in twentieth-century surveys of the philosophy of mathematics under the new names logicism, intuitionism, and formalism' (Quine, 1953, 14). More recently, Dummett has argued (1959, 327) that formalism provides no genuine alternative to the Platonism of a logicist such as Frege: a formalist is simply a realist who concentrates his attention on formal proofs rather than mathematical objects. The real choice lies between Platonism and various forms of constructivism:

The philosophical problem of necessity is twofold: what is its source, and how do we recognize it? God can ordain that something shall hold good of the actual world; but how can even God ordain that something is to hold good in all possible worlds? We know what it is to set about finding out if something *is* true; but what account can we give of the process of discovering whether it *must* be true? According to conventionalism, all necessity is imposed by us not on reality, but upon our language; a statement is necessary by virtue of our having chosen not to count anything as falsifying it. Our recognition of logical necessity thus becomes a particular case of our knowledge of our own intentions. (Dummett, 1959, 328)

There are various degrees of constructivism in modern thought, including the extreme conventionalism of the later Wittgenstein; there are also many forms of modern Platonism, including the thoroughgoing realism of Frege. Platonism in modern times can take different forms by concentrating on sentences, by concentrating on their subjects, and by concentrating on their predicates. The most common form of realism is Platonism about sentences: the belief that necessary truths are true in virtue of states of affairs independent of the sentences expressing them, without necessarily being truths about any concrete or even abstract entity. Expressions of this form of Platonism can be found in Russell's philosophy of mathematics at certain periods. Platonism about subjects is the realism characteristic of authors such as Meinong: the belief that even non-existent objects must in some way be *given* in order to provide references for the subjects of sentences about them. Platonism of predicates is one strand of the Platonism of Frege: the theory that predicates, no less than subjects, have reference. Since the predicate—in its modern sense of a sentence with a name punched out of it—was first identified as such by Frege, Platonism of predicates was hardly possible before his time.

In the medieval controversy about universals it is difficult to make a distinction between Platonism of subjects and Platonism of predicates: in the Aristotelian tradition one and the same expression or term may appear as either subject or predicate, as 'man' appears both in 'Socrates is a man' and 'man is an animal'. Medieval realism is therefore realism about terms: and so perhaps was the Platonism of Augustine and Plato himself. Descartes believed in mathematical objects, such as the geometers' triangle; but the essences of these objects were nothing more nor less than the eternal truths of geometry; and so in Descartes for the first time we meet the modern Platonism of sentences.

Though Descartes was the first modern Platonist in the sense that he was the first person to believe in the existence, distinct from God, of eternal truths which are the standard of our mathematical knowledge, his Platonism cannot be set in contrast to constructivism. For conventionalism, as Dummett insisted, reduces knowledge of mathematics to knowledge of mathematicians' intentions. But Descartes's understanding of necessary truths shares this voluntarist feature: knowledge of mathematics is knowledge of the legislation of the divine mathematician.

Wittgenstein often made use of the notion of divine omniscience to highlight his extreme constructivism:

Suppose that people go on and on calculating the expansion of π; so God, who knows everything, knows whether they will have reached '777' by the end of the world. But can his *omniscience* decide whether they *would* have reached it after the end of the world? It cannot. I want to say: Even God can determine something mathematical only by mathematics. (Wittgenstein, 1956, 185)

Against this, Descartes could say that God does know whether three sevens occur in the infinite expansion of π because it is his decision which makes it so or not so: his omniscience is omniscience about his own intentions in the relevant respect. Similarly, to Dummett's question posed above, Descartes would reply that God can indeed ordain that something is to hold good in all possible worlds, and that to deny this is to subject him to necessity and fate like the false gods of the heathen.

Descartes's Platonic voluntarism, therefore, might be said to combine the features of both realism and constructivism as nowadays understood. But it is indeed difficult to render intelligible the eternal divine mathematical decrees which are to fulfil the role which the mathematicians' endorsement of conventions play in conventionalist philosophy of mathematics. For the mathematicians' conventions concern their future operations with symbols; and though God can perhaps be conceived of as speaking to human beings in human tongues he can hardly be imagined to make play with symbols in eternity before the creation of the world. The Cartesian view seems indeed to combine the most unacceptable features of Platonism with the most implausible elements in constructivism.

The rival medieval theory, on the other hand, can reasonably claim to be neither Platonist nor constructivist. It is in no sense constructivist because the truths of mathematics do not depend on the decisions of any will, human or divine. It is not Platonist because it is not committed to the existence of eternal mathematical or logical states of affairs distinct from the existence of God himself. The truths of logic and mathematics, on this view, are essentially truths about the limits of divine power; but the limits in question are not limits which are, as it were, imposed from outside.

In the present century, some intuitionist philosophers have written as if truths of mathematics are truths about the human mind. From this point of view, the medieval scholastic theory of these matters could be regarded as a theological version of intuitionism. A modern intuitionist does not believe that there is anything outside the human mind to which it must conform itself if it is to be correct in its mathematical judgements. Similarly, the medieval scholastics thought that logical and mathematical truths were known by God simply by knowing the powers of his own essence, and it was not in virtue of anything outside his mind that what was in his mind was true.

In one important respect, however, the medieval differed from any modern intuitionist. For an intuitionist there can be no such thing as the direct apprehension of a mathematical truth not mediated by the appropriate mathematical inference; whereas all medieval theologians rejected the idea that God's knowledge might be mediated by inference. They insisted that God's thought was not discursive, and did not proceed step by step; as Augustine said, 'God does not see things piecemeal, turning his gaze from side to side; he sees everything at once.' Taking this as his text, Aquinas argued (*S.Th.* Ia, 14, 7) that in God there was neither the discursiveness which consists in thinking of one thing after another nor the discursiveness by which knowledge of conclusions depends on knowledge of principles. For God, knowledge of axioms must be a mirror in which to see theorems, not a sign-post to point the way to them.

However that may be, some modern philosophers of religion have argued that the medieval tradition offers an account of mathematical truth which combines the advantages of realism with those of constructivism. Like realism, it insists that the truth of logic and mathematics is an objective matter quite independent of the human mind. Like constructivism, it can avoid the postulation of eternal, extra-mental, abstract entities. Some have even gone so far as to suggest that the well-known difficulties in realism could be combined with the well-known difficulties in constructivism to constitute a novel version of the proof of God's existence on the basis of the eternal truths.

To me it seems that it is futile to postulate the existence of God as a solution to problems in the philosophy of mathematics. The problems about the objectivity of mathematical truth simply return as problems about the limits on God's power: limits which—on the scholastic theory—are necessary and yet not constraining, nonvoluntary and yet not imposed upon God. These are problems which we shall have to consider in their own right when we come to discuss divine omnipotence.

On the other hand, however, the notion of divine omniscience as applied to logic and mathematics does not add to the problems that are internal to the philosophy of mathematics. If realism is correct, then while God's relationship to Platonic truths may be mysterious, it is no less mysterious how we humans can come to know them by means of the artful manipulation of symbols. On the other hand, if the constructivists are in the right, then God's knowledge of the *a priori* disciplines reduces to his knowledge of his creatures: in particular to his knowledge of the powers, activities, and decisions of human beings.

III. OMNISCIENCE AND EXPERIENCE

We turn now from God's knowledge of eternal truths to his knowledge of empirical matters. Modern post-Kantian philosophers draw a sharp boundary between the *a priori* and the *a posteriori*, with logic and mathematics on one side of the line, and physics and chemistry on the other. This sharp boundary has not always been drawn. Descartes gave the same treatment to the laws of motion as he did to the truths of logic and mathematics: they are all eternal truths whose unchangingness is due to the unchangeable will of God. Similarly, for Aquinas the crucial distinction is not between *a priori* knowledge and *a posteriori* knowledge but between knowledge of essences and knowledge of particular things and events. The great divide is between God's knowledge of necessary truths (whether the necessity is logical, metaphysical, or natural), and his knowledge of contingent truths such as matters of historical fact. It is principally because both Descartes and St. Thomas differed from us in their view of natural science that they differ from us in the importance of the boundary between *a priori* and empirical knowledge.

St. Thomas appears to have believed that everything that can be scientifically known consists of conclusions derived by syllogistic reasoning from self-evident propositions. The findings of any science could be laid out as a set of theorems in a deductive system whose axioms were either theorems of another science or self-evident propositions. Thus an individual's knowledge of a particular science, such as geometry, grammar, or astronomy, could be regarded as a single mental disposition which extended in its scope to all the theorems provable within the science (e.g. *S.Th.* Ia, IIae, 54, 4).

Aquinas held up as the ideal of scientific method an axiomatic system like Euclidean geometry. Knowledge of the essence of material substances, on this view, would be equivalent to knowledge of the axioms of a theory. The other natural properties of substances would be derivable from knowledge of the axioms by anyone who knew the axioms at all; they would be known immediately, by the very fact of knowing the axioms, by a divine being whose knowledge was non-discursive. On this view, omniscience about science would not differ in principle from omniscience about mathematics.

To us there seems a radical difference between theories of mathematics and those of empirical science. Any number of axiomatic theories may be internally consistent and compatible with each other; and only an appeal to the empirical facts can settle which is true of the actual universe. This is the case with Euclidean and non-Euclidean geometries; this was the case with the Ptolemaic and Copernican astronomies. This point was made already by Descartes, who said that the *a priori* derivation of effects from causes could only show the various ways in which God *could have* made the world; experience was necessary for us to know the way in which he did actually make the world. As he wrote in his *Principles of Philosophy*:

Starting from sensible effects and sensible parts of bodies, I have tried to investigate the insensible causes and particles underlying them. This may give us an idea of the possible constitution of Nature; but we must not conclude that this is the actual constitution. There might be two clocks made by the same craftsman, equally good time-keepers, and with absolutely similar outsides; and yet the train of wheels inside might be completely different. Similarly the supreme Craftsman might have produced all that we see in a variety of ways. I freely admit the truth of this; I shall think I have done enough if only what I have written is such as to accord accurately with all natural phenomena. (*Principles* IV, CCIV. AT VIII-1. 327; trans. Geach, 1966, 327)

Descartes's letters to Mersenne (17 May 1638) and to Morin (13 July 1638) show a firm grasp of hypothetico-deductive method. 'To ask for geometrical demonstrations in a field within the range of physics is to ask the impossible . . . if people simply say that they do not believe what I have written, because I deduce it from certain hypotheses which I have not proved, then they do not know what they are asking or what they ought to ask.'

But in Descartes, side by side with passages of this admirable kind, we find attempts to provide *a priori* proofs of empirical generalizations, such as the alleged proof of the laws of motion from the immutability of God.

From the age of Descartes up to recent times philosophers of science have insisted more and more on the scientific role of verification and falsification, of confirmation and refutation by experiment. The *a priori* model of science has been replaced by the hypothetico-deductive model. A scientific theory however consistent and elegant is worthless without empirical support.

This view of science raises a special difficulty for divine knowledge of scientific truths. If God is immaterial, and stands outside the world of experience, how can he know what can only be known by experiment and observation? God, it seems, must either be credited with experience or denied knowledge of empirical truths.

Let us investigate the first possibility. The Psalmist asked, 'Is the inventor of the ear unable to hear? The creator of the eye unable to see?' These rhetorical questions have been answered by Christian theologians with a firm 'Yes, he is unable.' When the Psalmist says that the eyes of the Lord are on the just, St. Thomas hastens to explain that this does not mean that God has eyes, since he has no body. 'Parts of the body are ascribed to God in the scriptures by a metaphor drawn from their functions. Eyes, for example, see and so when "God's eye" is spoken of, it means his power to see, though even his seeing is an intellectual and not a sensory activity.' (*S.Th.* Ia, 3, 1 and 3.)

Medieval Aristotelians believed that in order to see, hear, feel, taste, or otherwise sense it was essential to have a body. Since they unanimously denied that God had a body they had in consistency to deny that God had any senses or any sense-knowledge. Descartes, on the other hand, believed that it was possible for a person to persuade himself that he had no body though still having sensations of heat and light; he concluded that sensations, as mental events, were connected only contingently with the body. But even Descartes believed that one's sensations are in fact due to the operation of one's body. Neither the scholastics, therefore, nor Descartes, credited God with sensation.

The philosopher who perhaps came nearest to attributing sensation to God is Berkeley. If *esse* is *percipi,* then objects when perceived by no finite spirit must be kept in existence by God's perceiving them; therefore in God's mind, it seems, there must be ideas of all perceptible things. But the existence of such divine sense-data is denied by Philonous, in the *Third Dialogue.* Hylas objects that it would follow from his theory that God, the perfect spirit, suffers pain, which is an imperfection. Philonous replies:

That God knows or understands all things, and that he knows, among
other things, what pain is, even every sort of painful sensation, and
what it is for His creatures to suffer pain, I make no question. But that
God, though He knows and sometimes causes painful sensations in us,
can Himself suffer pain, I positively deny . . . such a being as [God]
cannot be affected with any painful sensation or indeed any sensation at
all. . . . No corporeal motions are attended with the sensations of pain
or pleasure in His mind. To know everything knowable is certainly a
perfection; but to endure or suffer or feel anything by sense is an imperfection. The former, I say, agrees to God, but not the latter. God knows,
or hath, ideas; but His ideas are not conveyed to him by sense as ours
are. (Berkeley, 1954, 88)

Scholars disagree whether this passage is consistent with
Berkeley's epistemology. The difficulty is this. All ideas are for
Berkeley ideas in the mind of God. Since among the ideas we
encounter are those of hot and cold, sweet and sour, then these
ideas are somehow in the mind of God. If God none the less does
not feel sensations then the possession of such ideas is insufficient
for sensation. But if this is so, then Berkeley's account of ordinary
human sensation is quite inadequate.

Whatever may be true of Berkeley, most theist philosophers
have denied that God has eyes or ears or any sense experience.
None the less they firmly believed that God could know intel-
lectually all the truths which we know by the use of our senses.
By looking at the fire I see that it is red; by feeling I discover it
is hot; by tasting I discover that sugar is sweet and by touch that
it is rough. All these truths about particular things God knows,
they argued, without using any senses or having any sense
experience.

This doctrine seems to many people very difficult to accept.
We have a strong inclination, reinforced by centuries of empiricist
philosophy, to feel that there is some irreducible element of knowledge in experience which cannot be known in any other way than
by sensation. A blind man, we feel, cannot really understand what
is meant by colour words. Of course, we make reports about our
sensations, but we are inclined to think that no report of a sensation can ever be a full report, and that there must always be
something that is unreportable. This feeling finds expression in
reflections such as: 'For all we know, what I call red is what you
call green and vice versa.' When I have a pain I may think that

only I can really know how intense my pain is, or even that I am in pain at all.

On this point, contemporary philosophy has made the notion of omniscience easier, rather than harder, to accept. For this natural feeling, this empiricist presumption, has recently been subjected to detailed criticism by Wittgenstein in his famous discussion of private language in the *Philosophical Investigations*. Wittgenstein argued that the feeling we have of the incommunicability of sensation is an illusion. Whatever we know about our own sensations we can tell other people; what cannot be shared with others is not a piece of knowledge. 'Only I can know my sensation' means either that others cannot *know* that I am (e.g.) in pain; or that others cannot *feel* my pain. If it means the former then it is obviously false; someone who sees me falling into flames and screaming as my body burns knows perfectly well that I am in pain. If it means the latter then it is true but trivial, and there is no question of knowledge here. If 'Only I can feel my pain' is meant as a logical truth, it reveals the connection between 'I' and 'my': *my* pain is precisely the pain which *I* feel. Equally, only I can sneeze my sneezes; my sneezes are the ones which I sneeze; but there is nothing specially occult about a sneeze.

To have a sensation is not the same thing as to be in possession of a piece of knowledge. We do, of course, acquire information by the senses, but whatever information we acquire by the senses can be reported to others provided that they possess the appropriate language; and whatever can be reported to others can be discovered by others without the use of the sense in question, and without having the sensation. A blind man cannot see things, but he can learn all the things which others can learn by seeing, if only by asking others. He can understand the language of colours in the sense that he can master every employment of colour language except the one which involves the use of his own eyes to see.

But sensation is not the same thing as the acquisition of information about sensible objects. The blind man can acquire the information, but he lacks the sense of sight. What is the distinction between the two? What is it that the sighted man can do and the blind man cannot? I know of no better way of making the distinction between sense-perception and information-gathering than the one Aristotle used in the *De Anima*, where he says 'where there is sense-perception there is also both pain and pleasure' (414a4). The information acquired through the senses, and the discriminations performed with their aid, may be acquired and performed by means other than the senses and indeed by agents other than living beings. A scanner might discover, and a computer tabulate, visual information about various human beings in order to sort them into categories according to their appearance. The visual features of landscapes can be catalogued by the kinds of apparatus used in lunar exploration. Such operations are not sense-perception because they occur without pleasure or pain: the human beings inventoried with all their statistics are not perceived as either beautiful or ugly, the landscapes strike neither terror nor awe.

Of course, not every sense-experience is either pleasant or painful; but a sense is essentially a faculty for acquiring information in a modality which admits of pleasure and pain. The distinction between the intellectual knowledge that p and the sensation that p is to be sought, as Aristotle said, in the different relationship of each mode of cognition to pain and pleasure understood in the widest sense. The traditional account of omniscience attributes to God the informational content of our perceptions without the hedonistic content. All the information which we can acquire by our senses is possessed by God but without the pleasure–pain modality which constitutes the acquisition of this information a form of sensation. If Wittgenstein is right, there is nothing incoherent in such a conception.

Just as it is not necessary to have a sensation in order to know what can be known by the senses, similarly, and more obviously, it is not necessary oneself to perform an experiment in order to know what can be known by experiment. The great majority of the scientific knowledge of even the most industrious scientist is constituted by the results of experiments which he did not himself perform. On an extreme operationalist view of the nature of scientific inquiry, the meaning of the terms used in the statement of scientific theories is itself dependent on experience, or the experiments which would verify them. But the general theory that the meaning of a proposition is its mode of verification has been too destructively criticized to present a serious difficulty for the idea that God can know without experiment the results which human beings need experiment to confirm and confute. The truth in operationalism—that theories to which no experiments are relevant are idle theories—is something which is in no way incompatible with the possibility of non-experimental knowledge of truths discoverable by experiment.

Nor need a philosopher have a theological axe to grind to defend such a type of knowledge. Chomsky has proposed that children are born with innate knowledge of certain hypotheses about the construction of grammar in natural languages. This theory involves postulating non-experimental knowledge of hypotheses which can be confirmed or confuted experimentally; for a grammar, on Chomsky's view, is an explanatory theory: a theory accounting for the fact that a speaker of a language will perceive, interpret, form, or use an utterance in certain ways and not in other ways (Chomsky, 1968, 23 ff.). Of course Chomsky's theory of innate competences is hotly debated, and I do not appeal to it as an established fact, but merely as a non-theological illustration of the idea that empirical, contingent truths may be known by non-experimental methods.

To possess empirical knowledge, I have argued, it is not necessary actually to have sense-experience. To know a scientific truth it is not necessary to have verified it, or even to have confirmed it, oneself. To know that it has been verified or confirmed is quite enough. By far the greater part of our knowledge of scientific facts, of our acceptance of scientific theories, is based on the testimony of others. So it is not impossible in principle for a God to know empirical truth without himself having experience. But no one supposes that God waits on our testimony to know these truths; he does not have to look up the encyclopedia or wait for the next issue of the *Scientific American* to learn what has been discovered. How does he know the truths of nature and empirical facts of experience?

The traditional answer can be summed up: he knows these truths by knowing his own will. More accurately: he knows which hypotheses are possible hypotheses by knowing his own essence and its powers; he knows which hypotheses are actual by knowing which he has willed to enact. Aquinas makes a distinction between 'knowledge of understanding' (*scientia intelligentiae*), which is grasp of possibility, and 'knowledge of vision' (*scientia visionis*), which is awareness of reality:

Whatever can be produced or thought or said by a creature and also whatever God himself can produce, all is known by God, even if it is not actually existing. In this sense it can be said that he has knowledge even of non-existing things. Yet we have to take account of a difference among things not actually existing. Some of them, although they are not now actually existent, either once were so or will be: all these God is said to know by knowledge of vision. . . . Other things there are which can be produced by God or by creatures, which yet are not, were not and never will be. With respect to these God is said to have not knowledge of vision, but knowledge of simple understanding. (*S.Th.* Ia, 14, 9)

In these terms God's understanding of hypotheses will be part of his knowledge of simple understanding; his knowledge of their actualization will be his knowledge of vision. To put it in terms of essences: his knowledge that water is H_2O will be part of his knowledge of understanding; his knowledge that there is such a thing as water, and how distributed, in what form, in what purity, and so on will be part of his knowledge of vision. But why is there such a thing as water? Directly or indirectly, Aquinas will answer, because God willed to create it. And so the knowledge of vision depends on God's decree to create.

'It is not because things are what they are', said Augustine (*De Trinitate*, XV, 13), 'that God knows them, it is because he knows them that they are what they are.' Aquinas comments on this text as follows: 'God's knowledge is the cause of things; for God's knowledge stands to all created things as the craftsman's to his products. . . . But a craftsman, like anyone exercising an intellectual skill, operates as a result of his own volition. So too, divine knowledge is a cause only in conjunction with divine will' (*S.Th.* Ia, 14, 8). God's knowledge, then, is the cause of things in the way in which an architect's design is a cause of the house he builds. Divine knowledge, so understood, is practical rather than theoretical knowledge. The ancient and medieval notion of practical knowledge, as has been remarked by Professor Anscombe, has been neglected in modern philosophy. We have a contemplative conception of knowledge as a state which must be judged as such by being in accordance with the facts.

Professor Anscombe sketches 'practical knowledge' thus:

Imagine someone directing a project, like the erection of a building which he cannot see and does not get reports on, purely by giving orders. His imagination (evidently a superhuman one) takes the place of the perception that would ordinarily be employed by the director of such a project. He is not like a man merely considering speculatively how a thing might done; such a man can leave many points unsettled, but this man must settle everything in a right order. His knowledge of what is done is practical knowledge. (Anscombe, 1963, 82)

Anscombe considers the objection, that the man does not really have knowledge of what the house is like, but only 'knowledge of what the house is like if his orders have been obeyed'. The knowledge would be the same, however, she maintains, even if the orders had not been obyed. 'If then my knowledge is independent of what actually happens, how can it be knowledge of what does happen? Someone might say that it was a funny sort of knowledge that was still knowledge even though what it was knowledge of was not the case' (1963, 82). Still, she maintains, it *is* knowledge, for if what is done and what is in the designer's mind differ, the mistake is in the execution, not in the mind.

Professor Anscombe has put philosophers in her debt by drawing attention to two different 'directions of fit' here. As she says, if the building differs from the architect's drawing then the mistake is in the building, not in the drawing. We may contrast this with the case where there is a difference between a plan in a guide-book and the building; there the mistake is in the plan. But Anscombe is surely wrong to suggest that the architect has knowledge of what has happened. To take another of her examples, a man may mean to press button A and press button B. Here too, the mistake is in the performance; but we cannot say that he *knows that* he is pressing button A. Practical knowledge cannot be knowledge of what is not the case.

Someone who makes a mistake does not know what he is doing, even when it is true that the mistake is a mistake in the performance. The truth in Anscombe's point, it seems to me, is that if someone does know what he is doing—e.g. if he means to press button A and is pressing button A—then he knows that he is pressing button A without observation; he needs no further grounds, reason, evidence, etc. in order to make his meaning to press button A constitute knowledge that he is pressing button A. For speculative knowledge, in general, at least three things need to be the case for it to be true that X knows that p: first, that X believes that p, second, that p be true, and third, that X has grounds, i.e. good reason, for believing that p. In the case of practical knowledge only the first two are necessary.

Thus it seems possible to explain how divine knowledge of the world can be *knowledge*, and yet be practical knowledge; we can make room for the idea that knowledge is based on nothing other than his will to create. In the case of God, there can be no possibility of mistake or of the failure of servant demiurges to carry out orders; there cannot be inadvertence as when one presses button A meaning to press button B; there cannot be recalcitrant material preventing the design from being realized, as might happen to a sculptor or an architect.

Aquinas says that God's knowledge of himself, and of possible creatures, is purely speculative; but his knowledge of actual creatures is both speculative and practical. But his speculative knowledge of creatures is not derived from its objects, as human knowledge is.

Human speculative knowledge, according to Aquinas, is derived by abstraction from the objects of the knowledge; but this is not part of the nature of speculative knowledge in itself but of the nature of human knowledge. In fact, it does not seem to be true that the knowledge we have of numbers is derived from things themselves, either by abstraction from experience or by intuition of numbers. Yet knowledge of mathematics is speculative knowledge if anything is.

Discussing divine foreknowledge, Origen once remarked that it is not because God knows that something is going to take place that it is going to take place, but vice versa. How can this be reconciled with the doctrine that God's knowledge is the cause of things? Aquinas replies by drawing the distinction between practical and speculative knowledge. In the case of God's practical knowledge we can say that things are as they are because God has knowledge plus the will that they should be so; it is true of God's speculative knowledge, on the other hand, that he knows that things are as they are because they are as he wills. There is a difference between the two kinds of knowledge even in the case of omniscience. A being who was omniscient but not omnipotent, and so could have his plans frustrated, would need more than practical knowledge as a foundation for speculative knowledge. Aquinas sums up thus:

Natural things stand in the middle between God's knowledge and ours: for we get our knowledge from natural things of which God is the cause through His knowledge. Hence, just as the knowable things of nature are prior to our knowledge and are the measure of it, so God's knowledge is prior to natural things and is the measure of them. In the same way a house stands in the middle between the knowledge of the architect who made it and that of a man who gets his knowledge of the house from the house itself once made. (*S.Th.* Ia, 8, 3)

IV. OMNISCIENCE, ETERNITY, AND TIME

The God of western theism is an eternal God. The eternity of God is commonly expressed, in the Old Testament and New Testament, as everlasting duration. God lives for ever: he always was and he always will be; there never was a time when he was not; there never will be a time when there is no God. Many theologians have taken God to be eternal in rather a different sense, holding that God's duration is not just an everlasting duration but is strictly speaking no duration at all. In the sixth century Boethius defined eternity as the total and simultaneous possession of unending life and since his time eternity has been commonly understood as timelessness.

The timelessness doctrine has appealed to many theologians as seeming to provide a solution to the problem of the nature of God's knowledge of future contingent events—God's knowledge of human future actions for instance. Thomas Aquinas (e.g. *S.Th.* Ia, 13, 14) makes use of the doctrine of God's timelessness for this purpose. Future contingents, he maintains, are indeterminate and so cannot be the object of any kind of knowledge, divine or human. Nevertheless God can know them because God does not see future contingent facts as being future but as being present; future contingents are present to God. It is, St. Thomas says, nearer the truth that to say that if God knows a thing then it is, than to say that if he knows it then it will be. I have argued elsewhere that this solution to the problem of future contingents is not satisfactory:

The whole concept of a timeless eternity, the whole of which is simultaneous with every part of time, seems to be radically incoherent. For simultaneity as ordinarily understood is a transitive relation. If A happens at the same time as B, and B happens at the same time as C, then A happens at the same time as C. If the BBC programme and the ITV programme both start when Big Ben strikes ten, then they both start at the same time. But, on St. Thomas' view, my typing of this paper is simultaneous with the whole of eternity. Again, on this view, the great fire of Rome is simultaneous with the whole of eternity. Therefore, while I type these very words, Nero fiddles heartlessly on. (1969a, 264)

The difficulties expressed in the above passage were presented long ago in the seventh chapter of Suarez's book *De Scientia Dei Futurorum Contingentium*. Having observed that Aquinas, Augustine, and Boethius think that presence or coexistence is both sufficient and necessary to explain God's knowledge of the future, Suarez insists that though temporal things coexist with the whole of eternity, because eternity coexists with all times, past, present, and future, yet these different times do not coexist with each other. God coexists now with one thing and now with another thing, without changing in Himself; like a tree standing motionless in a river which is successively present or adjacent to different masses of flowing water. The only sense in which things are eternally present to God is as objects of His knowledge. The statement of their presence therefore is a restatement of God's knowledge of the future, and not an explanation of it.

Arthur Prior, in a paper called 'The Formalities of Omniscience' (1962), argued that the effect of treating God's knowledge as timeless would be to restrict God's knowledge to those truths, if any, which are themselves timeless. For example, he says:

God could not, on the view I am considering, know that the 1960 final examinations at Manchester are now over. For this isn't something that he or anyone could know timelessly, because it just isn't true timelessly. It's true now but it wasn't true a year ago (I write this on 29 August 1960) and so far as I can see all that can be said on this subject timelessly is that the finishing date of the 1960 final examinations is an earlier one than the 29th August, and this is not the thing we know when we know that those examinations are over. I cannot think of any better way of showing this than one I've used before, namely the argument that what we know when we know that the 1960 final examinations are over can't be just a timeless relation between dates, because this isn't the thing we're pleased about when we're pleased the examinations are over.

Nelson Pike, in his book *God and Timelessness* (1970), considers the arguments used by Prior and other philosophers writing in similar vein, and claims that they have not in fact identified a range of facts that a timeless being could not know, but only certain forms of words that a timeless individual could not use when formulating or reporting his knowledge. We have not been given a reason for thinking that facts such as that which a temporal being can report by saying 'today is the First of May' could not be reported by a timeless being in statements free of temporal indexical expressions.

I shall not try to settle whether a timeless being could or could not know temporal facts. Since, as I have said, I think on independent grounds that the doctrine of a timeless person is an incoherent one, I am not greatly interested in deciding whether a timeless person could be omniscient or not. Moreover, I agree with the general conclusion of Pike's book, which is that the doctrine of the timelessness of God is theologically unimportant and inessential to the tradition of western theism.

Discarding the doctrine of timelessness, however, does not solve the problems about the relation between time and omniscience. As Norman Kretzmann has shown, problems in this area are generated not only by the doctrine of timelessness, but also by the doctrine of immutability, which is far more deeply entrenched in the tradition of western theism.

Kretzmann propounds an argument in seven propositions:

(1) A perfect being is not subject to change
(2) A perfect being knows everything
(3) A being that knows everything always knows what time it is
(4) A being that always knows what time it is is subject to change
(5) A perfect being is therefore subject to change
(6) A perfect being is therefore not a perfect being
(7) Ergo there is no perfect being.

A scholastic who had to reply to Kretzmann in a formal disputation might proceed as follows:

I distinguish your first proposition thus:
    A perfect being is not subject to real change, I agree.
    A perfect being is not subject to apparent change, I deny.
I counter-distinguish proposition 4:
    A being that always knows what time it is is subject to real change, I deny.
    A being that always knows what time it is is subject to apparent change, I agree.
With the given distinctions I deny your conclusion and reject your proof.

The case for a distinction between real and apparent change has been persuasively argued by Geach:

The only sharp criterion for a thing's having changed, is what we may call the Cambridge criterion (since it keeps on occurring in Cambridge philosophers of the great days, like Russell and McTaggart): the thing called 'x' has changed if we have 'F(x)' at time t' true, and 'F(x)' at time t1' false, for some interpretation of 'F', 't', and 't1'. But this account is intuitively quite unsatisfactory. By this account, Socrates would after all change by coming to be shorter than Theaetetus; moreover, Socrates would change posthumously (even if he had no immortal soul) every time a fresh schoolboy came to admire him; and numbers would undergo change whenever e.g. five ceased to be the number of somebody's children.

The changes I have mentioned, we wish to protest, are not 'real' changes; and Socrates, if he has perished, and numbers in any case, cannot undergo 'real' changes. I cannot dismiss from my mind the feeling that there is a difference here . . . Of course there is a 'Cambridge' change whenever there is a real change, but the converse is not true. (Geach, 1969, 71)

Geach's last two examples are unhappy: surely 'Jones minor admires Socrates' and 'Five is the number of Smith's children' are not to be regarded as predications about Socrates and Five respectively; but his first, venerable example is beyond reproach, and shows that not every change in the truth-value of a predication about an object is a genuine change in it.

The distinction, then, has been made out: we must turn to the counter-distinction. Must a being who knows the time be subject to real change, or only to apparent change? Kretzmann considers the objection that change in an object of knowledge does not entail change in the knower. To this he replies that to know a change in anything is to know first that p and then that not p, and this is a change:

Adopting 'it is now tn' as a convenient standard form for propositions as to what time it is, we may say of a being that always knows what time it is that the state of its knowledge changes incessantly with respect to propositions of the form 'it is now tn'. First, such a being knows that it is now $t1$ (and that it is not now $t2$), and then it knows that it is now $t2$ (and that it is not now $t1$). To say of a being that it knows something different from what it used to know is to say that it has changed.

H. N. Castañeda (1967, 213) has replied to Kretzmann in a paper which suggests the following line of argument. 'It is now *t*1' and 'It is not now *t*1' are not, despite appearances, related as *p* and *not-p*; because the time indicated by 'now' is different in each case. There is no more a contradiction here than if I say 'I am Kenny' and someone else says 'I am not Kenny.' What is expressed by these two propositions could be known by someone who is neither of us; and similarly what is expressed by the propositions 'It is now *t*1' and 'It is now *t*2' could be known by somebody who was outside either of the times in question.

Kretzmann indeed accepts that to take account of a change, e.g. to bear in mind that it is now 1970 and not 1969, is not to change one's mind. It is, however, he claims, still an exception to the doctrine of immutability, and sufficient to overturn the traditional doctrine; for that doctrine ruled out not only deterioration-changes, or changes of mind, but anything which was a matter of incomplete actualization.

However, changes in God's knowledge similar to that argued for by Kretzmann were regarded as compatible with divine immutability by Thomas Aquinas. In a passage from which Kretzmann quotes (*S.Th.* Ia, 14, 15), Aquinas asks whether God's knowledge is changeable. He answers no: his knowledge must be altogether invariable just as his substance is altogether unchangeable. But there is the following difficulty. Once, God knew that Christ was yet to be born. But now he does not know that Christ is yet to be born (*nasciturus*), because Christ is no longer yet to be born. Therefore God does not now know all that he once knew. And thus his knowledge seems to be changeable.

Aquinas's reply begins by proposing a solution that he considers mistaken: 'Nominalists in the past (*antiqui nominales*) said that the propositions "Christ is being born", "Christ is yet to be born", and "Christ has been born" are identical, on the grounds that all three refer to the same thing, namely the birth of Christ, so that it follows that God knows whatever he knew, because he now knows Christ born, which means the same as "Christ will be born".'

This position of the old nominalists seems to resemble that of many modern logicians, according to which in a logically perspicuous notation tensed propositions should be replaced by timeless propositions containing an explicit time-reference, so that 'It is raining now in Oxford' is replaced by 'It is (timelessly) raining at 11.00 a.m. on 18 June 1978 in Oxford'. Aquinas goes on to reject it as conflicting with Aristotle's position that the same sentence 'Socrates is seated' is true when he is seated, false when he rises:

It must be granted then that 'Whatever God knew, he knows' is not true if the reference is to propositions (*si ad enuntiabilia referatur*). But it does not follow that God's knowledge is changeable. There is no change in the divine knowledge through his knowing that one and the same thing at one time exists and at another does not; and in the same way, there is no change in the divine knowledge through his knowing that a certain proposition is at one time true, at another time false.

God's knowledge would thereby be changeable only if he knew propositions in the same way as we do.

Aquinas agrees, then, that God is mutable to the extent that if we take the object of knowledge in its propositional expression then it is false that whatever God knew he knows; that is, we can formulate propositions such that 'God knows that *p*' is true at one moment and false at another; as Aquinas's example shows, the propositions are not necessarily about the time, they can be any significantly tensed propositions. But this, Aquinas claims, involves no real change in God because God does not think in propositions as we do. God's knowledge cannot change either by his changing his opinion on a topic, or by the truth of the matter changing while his opinion remains unaltered.

Aquinas's solution to the difficulty, like Castañeda's response to Kretzmann considered earlier, depends on the possibility of making a distinction between an item of knowledge and the way in which the knowledge is expressed. Pieces of knowledge are no doubt in general identified and individuated by their expression in language—this is something to which Aquinas would agree, since he believed both that knowledge was a disposition or state of mind (a *habitus*) and that dispositions were identified by the acts in which they were exercised or manifested (*S.Th.* Ia, IIae, 54, 2). But this does not necessarily mean that each item of knowledge has only one possible expression in language. Can it then be possible for two people A and B to have the same item of knowledge, but for there to be a way of expressing that knowledge which is open to A and not to B?

When we put the question in this way there is an immediate

and obvious answer. If A and B look out of the window at the rain, and A speaks only French and B speaks only English, they both possess the same item of information that it is raining, but A cannot express it by saying 'It is raining', and B cannot express it by saying 'Il pleut'. But this answer does not take us very far. Some philosophers make a distinction between sentences and propositions, and say that 'It is raining' and 'Il pleut' are two different sentences but are (or express) only a single proposition, and that in general synonymous sentences in different languages do not add up to more than one proposition. Aquinas's solution to the problem about omniscience demands that a single item of knowledge should be capable not only of expression in different sentences, but also in different propositions.[1]

If we count propositions by counting synonymous sentences, then it is clear that 'I am tired' and 'You are tired' are two different propositions. ('Je suis fatigué' would earn poor marks as a translation of 'You are tired'). If we understand propositions in this way, it is very natural to say that a single proposition may express two different items of knowledge (when you say 'You are tired' to me, and I say 'You are tired' to you, we are not each saying the same thing about the same person) and that one and the same item of knowledge can be expressed by two different propositions (as when I say to you 'I am tired' and you say to me 'You are tired').[2] Moreover, it may be that an item of knowledge which can be expressed by one person in a certain proposition can only be expressed by another in a quite different proposition. For instance, I know, as Boswell knew, that Dr. Johnson was a great lexicographer; but, not having had the pleasure of being acquainted with the Doctor, I cannot express that knowledge, as Boswell could, by saying

[1] Aquinas's use of *oratio* versus *enuntiabile* seems to correspond to the distinction between *sentence* and *proposition* sketched above.

[2] Some philosophers draw a distinction between propositions and statements. Thus E. J. Lemmon (1966, 87 ff.) suggests that we regard two propositions of subject-predicate form as making the same statement if the subject of each proposition has the same reference and the predicate the same extension. A statement, so defined, seems a rather strange entity. For instance the two propositions, 'Richard Nixon is a greater philosopher than Plato and Aristotle put together' and 'The Republican presidential candidate in the 1972 election was a politician wholly above reproach', would make the same statement, since the subjects refer to the same person and the extension of both predicates is the null class. Certainly my notion of an item of information differs from the notion of a statement, since unlike the latter it is not supposed to be identifiable in any merely extensional manner.

'You are a great lexicographer.' This seems to support the suggestion that there can be items of knowledge which an unchanging God can possess which nevertheless cannot be expressed by Him in ways in which a changing temporal being could and would express them.

Now can the distinction between an item of knowledge and the propositions which express it permit a solution to Kretzmann's problem along the lines suggested by Aquinas and Castañeda? If propositions are identified in the way suggested above, then it is clear that many propositions are significantly tensed: 'It will rain' is a very different proposition from 'It was raining', since one but not the other could be regarded as a translation of 'pluebat'. If Aquinas's account is correct, then a difference of tenses must be regarded as an instance of a difference of expression involving no difference in the knowledge expressed, so that 'It will rain' uttered before a particular shower and 'It rained' uttered after can express a single item of information.

Some philosophers believe that all that we now say by the use of tenses could equally well be said in a language which contained no tenses, but whose sentences continued timeless verbs plus an explicit temporal reference or quantification over times. Thus a sentence 'It will rain' uttered at time $t1$ would on this view have to be understood as expressing a proposition to the following effect: at some time t later than $t1$ it rains (timelessly). A. N. Prior has argued (1957, 1967, and 1968) that this reduction of tenses to times is impossible. For instance, the sense of 'It will rain' could only be caught by an analysis such as 'At some time later than t it rains, and $t1$ *is now*'; and '$t1$ is now' cannot in its turn be given a timeless analysis.[1] If tensed sentences could be reduced to tenseless sentences containing quantification over times, then there would of course be no difficulty in admitting that their content could be known by an unchanging, and even a timeless, being. But since they cannot, the difficulty remains.

Neither Castañeda nor Aquinas is committed to the elimination of tensed expressions: none the less they claim to have a solution to the difficulty. Castañeda's solution to Kretzmann's problem is

---

[1] 'Now' does not mean e.g. 'the time of utterance of this sentence' as is shown by the inscription on the monument in the desert 'Say, O stranger, if thou canst, the time of my inscribing'—an inscription which does not mean 'what is the time now?'. (I believe I owe this example to Professor P. T. Geach.)

well summarized by Richard Swinburne, who accepts it as satisfactory, in the following passage:

A knows on 2 October the proposition 'it is now 2 October'. Surely B on 3 October can know that A knew what he did on 2 October. How can B report his knowledge? By words such as 'I know that A knew yesterday that it was then 2 October.' How can we report B's knowledge? As follows: B knew on 3 October that on the previous day A knew that it was then 2 October. Hence . . . B knows on 3 October what A knew on 2 October, although B will use different words to express the latter knowledge. In reporting B's knowledge of this item, we need a different referring expression to pick out the day of which being 2 October is predicated; but what is known is the same. . . . What A knows on 2 October and B knows on 3 October is that a certain day which can be picked out in many and various ways, according to our location in time, as 'today' or 'yesterday' or 'the day on which A thought that it was 2 October' (or even as '2 October') is 2 October. (Swinburne, 1977, 166)

If this is correct, then an unchanging being can know the time and date and all that we know and express is tensed propositions.

The essential elements of the solution are these. 'Today is Friday' (uttered on Friday) and 'Yesterday was Friday' (uttered on Saturday) are indeed two different propositions; but both express the same item of knowledge. God's knowledge is not expressed in propositions, and so he can know the same item of knowledge permanently and unchangingly. It is only because we are temporal changing beings that we have to express the one item of knowledge first in one proposition and then in another.

The solution, however, is not wholly satisfactory. In the first place it is incorrect to regard 'Today' in 'Today is Friday' as a referring expression picking out a day; it is no more a referring expression than is the 'it' in the synonymous sentence 'It is Friday today'. Secondly, and more importantly, 'Today is Friday' on Friday does not express the same knowledge as 'Yesterday was Friday' on Saturday. This can be proved by the argument used by Prior in the passage quoted at the beginning of this chapter: what I am glad about when I am glad that today is Friday is not at all necessarily the same thing as what I am glad about when I am glad yesterday was Friday. Perhaps Friday is payday, on which I always go out for a massive carouse with my friends: when it is Friday, I am glad today is Friday, but during Saturday's hangover

I am not at all glad that yesterday was Friday. Moreover, the power that the knowledge that it is Friday gives me on Friday (e.g. the power to keep engagements made for Friday) is quite different from the very limited power which is given me by Saturday's knowledge that yesterday was Friday if unaccompanied by the realization on Friday that it was indeed Friday.

It was an essential part of Aquinas's reconciliation of omniscience with immutability that God's knowledge was not exercised in thinking of, or uttering, propositions. For if God did indeed think in propositions, then knowledge such as knowledge of the time would undoubtedly involve change: the change, for instance, from thinking the true proposition 'Now it is 12.50' to thinking the true proposition 'Now it is 12.51.' But there can be no general objection to the idea that someone may have a piece of knowledge without uttering, even in the privacy of the imagination, any proposition which expresses that knowledge: the great majority of the things we know at any given time is not, and could not all be, so expressed. What we know we *can* (barring impediments such as aphasia) express in propositions: but we are willing to attribute knowledge even to beings without language, as when we say that a cat knows that there is a mouse in the corner behind the skirting-board. There is not, to be sure, in the case of divine knowledge any obvious analogy to the behaviour of animals on the basis of which we attribute animal knowledge; and this lack of analogy is not a trivial matter. But we might indeed imagine God giving even linguistic expression to knowledge of the time. We could perhaps conceive of a cosmic timekeeper on the model of the GPO speaking clock: a voice from the clouds that said, with unfailing regularity, sentences of the form, 'Thus saith the Lord: at the third stroke it will be 12.52 precisely' followed by three crashes of thunder.

Even such a fantasy, it seems, would not give substance to the idea that a changeless being might know the time. Merely creating, at the beginning of the world, a cosmic apparatus of the appropriate kind, would not by itself constitute knowledge of the time: the GPO engineers and the voice who recorded the speaking clock are not, by virtue of that very fact, apprised of the correct time at every moment of the day. Whereas if we attribute to God in addition awareness of what the cosmic clock is saying at any given moment, we merely reawaken in fantastic form all the difficulties about changeless awareness of a changing world which we have been considering.

If a changeless being cannot know the time, then it cannot know either what is expressed by tensed propositions. Knowing that 'Christ will be born' is true (roughly) throughout the years BC and that 'Christ has been born' is true throughout the years AD will not—*pace* Aquinas—enable one to know which of these two propositions is true *now*, unless one also knows the date. Kretzmann's difficulty, then, is a serious one: it does not simply point to a tiny frivolous exception to an otherwise coherent claim that God knows everything that there is to be known. A believer in divine omniscience must, it seems, give up belief in divine immutability.[1]

---

[1] In an interesting appendix Kretzmann (1966) claims that human self-consciousness as well as knowledge of time presents a difficulty for omniscience. Each of us knows certain propositions about himself that no other person can know. When I know that Kretzmann is the author of 'Omniscience and Immutability' I do not know the same item of knowledge as Kretzmann expresses by saying 'I am the author of "Omniscience and Immutability"', because Kretzmann, if he became amnesiac, might lose the one piece of information while retaining the other. In his exposition Kretzmann alludes to Descartes: but his argument need not presuppose a Cartesian framework. Writing from a Wittgensteinian background Professor Anscombe maintains that each of us can utter a genuine proposition 'I am this thing here', pointing to his or her own body (Anscombe, 1975). If this is a genuine proposition it can presumably be known—but by each of us only in his own case. If Anscombe's view of first-person self-consciousnes is correct, then Kretzmann's appendix does present another counter-instance to the claim that it is coherent to suppose that there is an omniscient being; but unlike the difficulty about change and time this seems to me to call for only a trivial restatement of the traditional doctrine.

PART TWO

FOREKNOWLEDGE

V. FOREKNOWLEDGE AND INDETERMINISM

If the argument of the preceding chapter was correct, an immutable being cannot know what we know by means of tensed propositions. If, then, there is a God who knows all that we know, he must be subject in some degree to change. Some theists welcome this conclusion: others regard it as incompatible with traditional conceptions of God. Geach, for instance, has written:

Only an unchanging God can be coherently regarded as causing everything other than himself; it would be merely arbitrary to say that of two mutable beings one required a cause, the other did not. We may dismiss the question 'Who made God?' if we regard God as everlasting and changeless; for only where there is some beginning or some change can there be question of a cause; to dismiss the question if we regard God as changeable is, in Schopenhauer's words, to think you can pay off an argument like a cab when it has taken you as far as you choose to go. Process theology is not a live option. (Geach, 1977, 42)

No less entrenched in traditional theism than the attribute of immutability is the doctrine that God knows everything that human beings will do. God's foreknowledge of future human deeds and misdeeds seems indeed more fundamental to religious theism than any general omniscience about abstract or scientific truths. If human actions are free, the doctrine of foreknowledge meets special difficulties in addition to the general difficulties about divine knowledge of the future which we considered in the last chapter— difficulties which will not necessarily disappear even if the doctrine of immutability is jettisoned. This chapter and the next will be devoted to these special problems.

The problem of reconciling divine foreknowledge with human freedom takes different forms corresponding to different views of the nature of freedom. Some philosophers and theologians regard free actions as being, by definition, undetermined in advance: for them the problem of accounting for divine foreknowledge is particularly acute. Other thinkers regard freedom as being compatible with determinism: for them the problem of divine foreknowledge is comparatively easy to solve, and the difficulty lies in explaining how something which is determined in advance can be a genuinely free action. In the present chapter I shall discuss the problem of divine foreknowledge as it presents itself from an indeterminist viewpoint, and in the next chapter I shall discuss solutions of the problem which depend on a reconciliation between freedom and determinism.

On the indeterminist view, any future-tensed proposition about free human action must be contingent: it must be capable of turning out either true or false. If it were necessarily true, then the action predicted by the proposition could not be free, but would be determined. But then can a contingent proposition about the future be true at all, or must we say that as long as it is capable of turning out either true or false it lacks a truth-value altogether? This question was first raised long ago by Aristotle.

In the ninth chapter of the *De Interpretatione,* Aristotle appears to argue that if every proposition is either true or false—including future-tensed propositions about singulars like 'There will be a sea-battle tomorrow'—then everything happens necessarily and there is no need to deliberate or to take trouble. 'For there is nothing to prevent someone's having said ten thousand years beforehand that this would be the case, and another's having denied it; so that whichever of the two it was true to say then, will be the case of necessity.' On the most common interpretation, Aristotle's argument is meant as a *reductio ad absurdum.* If future-tensed propositions about singulars are already true, then fatalism follows: but fatalism is absurd; therefore, since many future events are not yet determined statements about such events are not yet true or false, though they later will be. (See Ackrill, 1963, 140.)

Whether or not this is the correct interpretation of Aristotle (it is questioned, for instance, in Anscombe, 1956), his doctrine was thus understood in the Middle Ages, e.g. by Boethius, Aquinas, and Ockham.[1] This view, that future-contingent propositions have no truth-value, or perhaps a third truth-value between true and false, is the most extreme form of indeterminism. It was not a popular view in the Middle Ages, because of the limits it appears to place on God's foreknowledge and ability to predict the future. Clearly, if future-contingent propositions are not true, then not

---

[1] For a compact history of recent exegesis of *De Interpretatione 9*, see Celluprica, 1977.

even God can know them, since only what is true can be known. But the Bible is full of prophecies of future events which depend on the free choices and decisions of human beings; but if future contingents lack a truth-value, then these prophecies are untrue, or were untrue when uttered. It is therefore not surprising that when Peter de Rivo at Louvain in the fifteenth century defended the view that future contingents lack a truth-value he came into conflict with the highest ecclesiastical authorities. (Baudry, 1950, 89 ff.) Five propositions of his were condemned by Pope Sixtus IV in the bull *Ad Christi vicarii* as being scandalous and wandering from the path of Catholic faith. The two final ones read thus: 'For a proposition about the future to be true, it is not enough that what it says should be the case: it must be unpreventably the case. We must say one of two things: either there is no present and actual truth in the articles of faith about the future, or what they say is something which not even divine power could prevent.' The other three condemned propositions were ones in which Peter tried to find proofs in Scripture for this three-valued system of logic (Denzinger, 1952, nn. 719–23).

In our own time a view similar to Peter de Rivo's has been defended by Geach. It is a mistake, Geach argues, to accept the picture of the future as a set of events which, though they have not yet happened, are already *there*, but in some way invisible to us. The future consists of nothing more than certain actual trends and tendencies in the present that have not yet been fulfilled. The past, though no more presently actual than the future, does exist in the sense that past objects can be named and can therefore be quantified over. But not-yet-existent objects cannot be named, even though we can pick names *for* them: there is an ineradicable generality in certain statements about the future. Geach, like de Rivo, rejects the idea that Jones's dying of cancer in 1978 is necessary and sufficient for Smith's statement 'Jones will die of cancer in 1978', made in 1977, to be true. But de Rivo regards Jones's subsequent death as insufficient: it must also have been unpreventable in 1977 if Smith's statement was to be true. Geach, it appears, regards the subsequent death as unnecessary: for he reduces statements about the future to statements about what is going to happen; and of course it may have been true in 1977 that Jones was going to die of cancer—the diagnosis of terminal cancer was perfectly correct—and yet, as it turned out, the moribund Jones was run over by a bus on his way to the nursing home and did not die of cancer after all.

Geach does not deny that God is omniscient about the future. If future-tensed propositions are true only when they correspond to actual unfulfilled tendencies, then there is no problem about saying that God knows all true future propositions. Whatever we can say is going to be, we can also say is known by God. However, this solution to the problem seems only a Pyrrhic victory over the difficulties. It preserves the doctrine of omniscience (the doctrine that, for all p, God knows that p if and only if p) but only at the cost of greatly restricting the range traditionally ascribed to God's foreknowledge. So far as I can see, on this view of the matter it would be quite wrong to say that in 1918 God already knew that Hitler would later on massacre six million Jews. And anyone who did not know that in 1918 must have been ignorant of a very great deal about the way the world now is in 1978.

Perhaps Geach does not wish to restrict the scope of divine knowledge to so great an extent, because he maintains that God knows the future not only by knowing present tendencies in the world and present intentions of human beings but also, and principally, by knowing his own intentions about a world over which he has absolute control. I shall consider this suggestion in a moment: but I wish first to mention the theory to which Geach explicitly sets himself in opposition, the theory that God knows future events by seeing them as they are in themselves.

St. Thomas Aquinas maintained that future-contingent propositions could be true; but they could not, qua future, be known, whether to man or God. They were known to God because compresent to him in eternity: he knows them in their presentness and not as future. As I said in the last chapter, the concept of eternity presupposed here seems an incoherent one; and, as Geach says, the type of knowledge ascribed to God seems to involve either misperception or a self-contradictory feat. 'Misperception is involved if God is supposed to perceive what really is future not *as* future but as present: flat self-contradiction, if what God sees is *both* future *and* simultaneously (since in itself it is just as God sees it) also present' (Geach, 1977, 57). If we were to construct a descending scale of indeterminism, Aquinas's theory would come next below that of Peter de Rivo. Propositions about future free actions would be indeterminate for us, but determinate for God; they would, as it were, lack a truth-value in time but possess one in eternity.

Though Aquinas's theory seems, to me as to Geach, to be fundamentally incoherent, one of the arguments which he offers in support of it is a very powerful one, which deserves detailed consideration. It runs as follows. What is entailed by a necessary proposition is itself necessarily true. But from 'God has always known that there will be a sea-battle tomorrow' there follows 'There will be a sea-battle tomorrow.' But 'God has always known that there will be a sea-battle tomorrow', if true, is necessarily true, because it concerns the past and the past is now determined. Hence 'There will be a sea-battle tomorrow', if true, is necessarily true. The argument can be generalized to show that if God knows the future, the future is not contingent. Aquinas presents this argument as an objection to the thesis that God knows future contingents: in the end he accepts the conclusion but attempts to disarm it by claiming that a contingent event, as it comes to God's knowledge, is not future but present, and as present is necessary, since the present, like the past, is what it is and is beyond anyone's power to alter.

Anyone who finds Aquinas's account unacceptable can only defend divine foreknowledge of future contingents by rejecting one of the premisses of Aquinas's argument. It seems undeniable that what is entailed by a necessary proposition is itself necessary: so critics of Aquinas have fastened on the claim that 'God has always known that there will be a sea-battle tomorrow' is necessarily true. First of all, it is clear that the proposition is not logically necessary: if 'There will be a sea-battle tomorrow' is not a logical truth, then neither is 'God knows that there will be a sea-battle tomorrow.' But this truth will not suffice to protect the doctrine of divine foreknowledge of future free actions as understood by an indeterminist: for it is a cardinal point of indeterminism that there is a certain necessity which attaches to past and present which does not attach to the future, a necessity which is quite distinct from the timeless necessity of logic. The point is not well made by saying that we can alter the future and not the past; for if the future is what will happen (as opposed to what is going to happen and may yet be prevented from happening), then the future can no more be changed than the past: whatever changes of plan we may make, the future is whatever takes place after all the changes are made. The point that the indeterminist wishes to make is that we can bring about the future, but not bring about the past: our present activity may have an effect on what will happen, but cannot have an effect on what has happened. (See Kenny, 1969, 267.) If this is so, then Aquinas's difficulty appears to remain. Since God's knowledge that there will be a sea-battle is something in the past, nothing we now do can have any effect on it. But since that knowledge entails that there will be a sea-battle, nothing we can now do can have any influence on whether there will or will not be a sea-battle tomorrow.

It might be questioned whether 'God has always known that there will be a sea-battle tomorrow' is really, as it appears to be, a proposition about the past. Some have thought that it was a proposition infected with futurity: a compound of the genuinely past-tensed proposition 'God has always believed that there will be a sea-battle tomorrow' and of the future-tensed proposition 'There will indeed be a sea-battle tomorrow.' Being a future-infected proposition, some have argued, it is not determined, or necessary, in the way that genuinely, undilutedly, past-tensed propositions are. Thus, the fact that it entails 'There will be a sea-battle tomorrow' does not mean that it cannot be a contingent fact that there will be a sea-battle tomorrow. Thus divine fore-knowledge is compatible with a contingent future.

In our time, Nelson Pike has shown that this escape route is not open. Any difficulty which arises from 'God has always known that there will be a sea-battle tomorrow' arises equally with 'God has always believed that there will be a sea-battle tomorrow.' Suppose, Pike says, that Jones mowed his lawn last Saturday. Then, eighty years earlier, God, if he is omniscient, believed that Jones would mow his lawn on Saturday. On Saturday Jones did not have the power to perform an act the performance of which would require that God would not have believed as he in fact believed eighty years earlier. For by the time Saturday arrived, God's belief was well into the past. Nothing that Jones was able to do on Saturday could have had the slightest bearing on whether God held a certain belief eighty years earlier. Therefore, if God is omniscient, Jones was not able not to mow his lawn on Saturday, and therefore did not mow his lawn freely. (Pike, 1970, 58.)

This difficulty was anticipated in the Middle Ages by John Duns Scotus. Scotus rejected, as we have done, Aquinas's presentiality theory of divine foreknowledge. Scotus's own account makes the basis of God's knowledge of future contingents God's knowledge of his own will. Take a proposition such as 'Adam will eat the apple.' When the divine mind considers this proposition in eternity, prior to any divine decision, it apprehends it as neuter (neither true nor false) just as I apprehend the proposition 'The total number of the stars is an even number.' But after the decree of God's will, the proposition begins to be determinately true, as it was not before. Once it thus becomes determinately true, it can be known by God. However, it remains a contingent truth, since the decrees of God's will are not necessary but contingent.

Among the objections which Scotus presents against his own account there occurs the following:

'God thinks I will sit tomorrow, and I will not sit tomorrow, therefore God is mistaken' is a valid argument. Similarly, therefore, the following is a valid argument: 'God thinks I will sit tomorrow, and it is possible for me not to sit tomorrow, therefore it is possible for God to be mistaken.' The first argument is clearly valid, because someone who believes what is not the case is mistaken. The second argument is valid if the first is, because just as the unmodalised conclusion follows from the two unmodalised premisses, the modalised conclusion follows from one unmodalised and one modalised premise. (Scotus, VI, 403)[1]

The objection is clearly essentially the same as Pike's argument. I do not fully understand the answer which Scotus gives to the objection: but elsewhere in his writings he puts his finger on the subtle fallacy which it involves. (See *Ordinatio*, 1 dist. 39; Scotus, V, 424.) The argument depends upon the following principle:

If to ϕ is to ψ, and I can ϕ, then I can ψ.

This seems harmless enough, but in fact is false, if it is considered as having unrestrictedly general application.

There are many cases where I can ϕ, but will not. In such cases, there will be descriptions ψ of ϕ-ing which will describe it in terms of the fact that I am in fact, not going to ϕ. Thus, let us suppose

---

[1] 'Quia sequitur Deus novit me sessurum cras, et non sebedo cras, ergo Deus decipitur; igitur a simili sequitur Deus novit me sessurum cras, et possum non sedere cras, ergo Deus potest decipi. Prima est manifesta, quia credens illud quod non est in re, decipitur. Probo ex hoc quod consequentia teneat, quia sicut ad duas de inesse sequitur conclusio de inesse, ita ex una de inesse at altera de possibili sequitur conclusio de possibili.'

that I am going to eat my cake. I can, if I want, have my cake, but I am not going to have my cake, I am going to eat it. Given the facts of the case, to have my cake would be to have it and eat it too. But I can, if I want, have it. So, if the principle is valid, I can have my cake and eat it too. Now Pike's argument depends on the principle 'If not mowing the lawn is bringing it about that God held a false belief, then if Jones can not mow the lawn, Jones can bring it about that God held a false belief.' Clearly, the description 'bring it about that God held a false belief' is a description ψ of ϕ-ing (not mowing the lawn) in terms of the fact that Jones is, in fact, going to mow the lawn. It is therefore a case where the principle does not hold.

Scotus's solution to this difficulty seems to me a genuine one, which throws light on problems of freedom and determinism even outside the theological context in which he expounded it (see Kenny, 1976, 56). But his account of the *basis* of divine knowledge of creatures' free actions—God's knowledge of his own intentions —seems to be open to a more fundamental objection, clearly propounded by William Ockham. Ockham writes:

I ask, whether the decision of the creature's will necessarily results from the decision of the divine will or not. If it does, then the will must be acting of necessity, just as fire does, and desert and guilt are done away with. If not, then whether p or not-p will be the case cannot be known prior to the decision of the creature's will: the decision of the divine will does not suffice, since the creature's will will have the power to decide in the opposite sense. Therefore, since the decision of the creature's will is not something existing from all eternity, God has not had from eternity knowledge of the matters left unsettled prior to the creature's decision. (Ockham, 1945, 14; 1969, 49)

But Ockham was himself unable to present any coherent account of divine foreknowledge. 'I maintain', he says, 'that it is impossible to express clearly the way in which God knows future contingents. Nevertheless, it must be held that he does so, but contingently. This must be held because of the pronouncements of the Saints.'

Ockham's objection to Scotus can be applied to the Scotist account of divine foreknowledge put forward in our own day by Geach. Geach imagines God and man as engaged in a game of chess:

God is the supreme Grand Master who has everything under his control.

Some of the players are consciously helping his plan, others are trying to hinder it; whatever the finite players do, God's plan will be executed; though various lines of God's play will answer to various moves of the finite players. God cannot be surprised or thwarted or cheated or disappointed. God, like some grand master of chess, can carry out his plan even if he has announced it beforehand. 'On that square,' says the Grand Master, 'I will promote my pawn to Queen and deliver checkmate to my adversary': and it is even so. No line of play that finite players may think of can force God to improvise: his knowledge of the game already embraces all the possible variant lines of play, theirs does not. (Geach, 1977, 58)

This striking picture embodies faithfully some familiar doctrines of predestination: however God's sinful human opponents may struggle, at the last they will either die repentant and reach Heaven or die in sin and descend to Hell, and in either case they will be doing what God has willed from eternity that they should do. But the image in no way captures the doctrines of omniscience or foreknowledge. When a Grand Master plays a novice he may foresee every possible move, but he does not foresee which moves will actually be made: even if the game goes no further than Scholar's Mate there are many different pairs of opening moves the Scholar can make. To make Ockham's point: if the moves of the creator do not necessarily determine the moves of the creature, they do not provide a basis for foreknowledge. God's decrees will enable him to foresee his creatures' actions only if every move in the game of life is a forced move.

The Scotist account of divine foreknowledge seems tenable only if human free actions are in some way predetermined. Yet Scotus held a theory of creaturely freedom which appears strongly indeterminist. Some philosophers, anxious to reconcile freedom with determinism, have claimed that in order to act freely it is not necessary to have the power to act in any way otherwise than we do; it is sufficient to be able to do what we will. Scotus does not adopt any such view. If one does X freely, he maintained, then at the very moment of doing X one must have the power not to do X. Ockham found this incredible. If I am doing X freely at t, he maintained, then perhaps up to time t I had the power not to do X, and perhaps I have the power not to do X at $t+1$, but at t itself I cannot have the power not to do X. He seems to have thought that the proposition:

While I am doing X I have the power not to do X

entailed the obvious absurdity:

I have the power to not-do-X-while-I-am-doing-X (Ockham, 1945, 32 ff.; 1969, 71 ff.).

But of course it does not, just as 'Necessarily, if p then p' does not entail 'If p, then necessarily p.' This dispute, begun by Scotus and Ockham, was to have a long future.

All medieval scholastics, however much they may have differed in the accounts they gave of divine foreknowledge of free action, were in agreement both that human beings enjoyed freedom of the will, and that God foreknew all free actions. At the Reformation the area of disagreement was widened: among Protestants some, such as Luther, denied the freedom of the will; others, such as Sozzini, denied the universality of divine foreknowledge. Luther's teaching will be considered in the next chapter when we come to treat of determinist accounts of divine foreknowledge; Sozzini's theory of limited prevision has been propounded in a contemporary form by John Lucas in his book *The Freedom of the Will* (1970).

Lucas writes:

The real solution to the problem of God's omniscience is to be found by drawing a parallel with his omnipotence. Although God is able to do all things, we do not think he does do all things. . . . We allow that some things happen against God's will. . . . If God is prepared to compromise his omnipotence for the sake of human freedom, surely then he would be prepared to compromise his omniscience also. If he suffers his will to be confined in order that his creatures may have room to make their own decisions, he must allow his understanding to be abridged in order to allow men privacy to form their own plans for themselves. It seems to me entirely unobjectionable that God should limit his infallible knowledge as he does his power, in order to let us be independent of him. (Lucas, 1970, 75)

The notion of a voluntary self-limitation of divine power seems to me incoherent. Human beings who depend on bodily senses for their knowledge of the world can close their eyes and stop up their ears to prevent themselves coming to know things which they do not wish to know; but God's nature cannot be thought of as limited in the same way as fragile mortal organisms like ourselves. If the limitation of God's knowledge is a voluntary one, then the knowledge renounced by God must be knowledge which it is logically possible to have: hence Lucas's solution does nothing to solve the problem of how divine foreknowledge can be logically reconciled with future indeterminism. The parallel with omnipotence is misleading. It is no limitation on a power that it is not exercised: hence even an omnipotent being may have many powers which he does not exercise. It would equally be no limitation on omniscience to be in possession of knowledge which is not exercised, i.e. acted on; but the parallel to the non-possession of knowledge is not the non-exercise, but the non-possession, of powers; and that is indeed something which is incompatible with omnipotence.

The most sophisticated attempt to reconcile divine foreknowledge with human freedom indeterministically understood was that of the sixteenth-century Jesuit theologians Francesco Suarez and Luis de Molina.[1] These Jesuit theologians agreed with Ockham in rejecting Aquinas's and Scotus's accounts. They did believe there to be truth-values attached to future-contingent propositions, and unlike Ockham they offered a positive account of how God knew them. In their definition of freedom, they were in agreement with Scotus: 'That agent is called free which in the presence of all necessary conditions for action can act and refrain from action or can do one thing while being able to do its opposite.' This is the conception of freedom which became famous as liberty of indifference. (Molina, 1953, 14, 13, d2 n3.)

Ockham was wrong, Molina said, to affirm that at the moment of doing an action I am not free not to do it. Let us suppose that doing X at t is sinful. Then, on Ockham's view, the guilt of this sin cannot be incurred at t, since at t I am not capable of avoiding it. It must therefore be incurred immediately before t. But what does 'immediately before' mean? It cannot refer to an instant of time: there is no such thing as one instant immediately before another. It must therefore mean a preceding period of time, during which the sinner retained the ability not to sin. But if the sinner had freedom during that period, then he must have had freedom during the latter half of that period, and therefore he did not commit the sin during the first half of the period. We can divide the latter period in half once again, and conclude that the sin cannot have been committed during the first half of the latter half. Obviously, this pattern of argument can be repeated without

[1] An excellent contemporary account of Suarez's and Molina's theory is Adams, 1977.

end, and so we must conclude that the sin was not committed during any part of the period preceding the sinful action itself. The only way to avoid this regress is to agree with Scotus against Ockham that a free agent, at the time of the action itself, retains the power to act otherwise. (Molina, 1935, 208.)

Molina's account of God's foreknowledge of human action appeals to divine knowledge of counterfactual propositions. God knows what any possible creature would freely do in any possible circumstances: by knowing this and by knowing which creatures he will create and which circumstances he will himself bring about, he knows what actual creatures will in fact do. Molina made a distinction between three kinds of divine knowledge. First, there is God's natural knowledge, by which he knows his own nature and all the things which are possible to him either by his own action or by the action of free possible creatures. Then there is God's free knowledge: his knowledge of what will actually happen after the free divine decision has been taken to create certain free creatures and to place them in certain circumstances. Between the two there is God's 'middle knowledge': this is his knowledge of what any possible creature would do in any possible world.

Molina explains his theory of natural and middle knowledge thus:

God in his eternity knew by natural knowledge all the things that he could do: that he could create this world and infinitely many other worlds; that he could create this one at such and such a point of time or at any other one; . . . that he could create in this world the human beings that he had decided to create, or other human beings not identical with these; that he could so arrange this universe that there should be the opportunities and circumstances that have in fact arisen, or other opportunities and circumstances not identical with these; . . . that he could give each human being such and such a character, or a different character; and so for all the infinitely many other orders and combinations of things and circumstances which in his omnipotence he could bring about in this universe.

Moreverover, given his complete comprehension and penetrating insight concerning all things and causes, he saw what would be the case if he chose to produce this order or a different order; how each person, left to his own free will, would make use of his liberty with such-and-such an amount of divine assistance, given such and such opportunities, temptations and other circumstances, and what he would freely do, retaining all the time the ability to do the opposite in the same opportunities temptations and other circumstances. (Molina, 1935, 239)

What Molina calls 'orders of things and circumstances' is akin to what philosophers since Leibniz have called 'possible worlds'. God's knowledge of what will happen in the actual world, on Molina's theory, is based on his knowledge of what creatures will do in any possible world, plus his own knowledge of which possible world he is going to bring about. Before creating Adam and Eve God knew that Eve would succumb to the serpent's temptation and that Adam would succumb to Eve's temptation. He knew this because he knew all kinds of counterfactuals about Adam and Eve: he knew what they would do in all possible worlds. He knew, for instance, whether Adam, if tempted directly by the serpent and not by Eve, would still have eaten the forbidden fruit.

In aid of this ingenious solution, Molina had first to prove that God knew the counterfactual conditionals which are the objects of middle knowledge. For this purpose he searched the Scriptures and produced three texts. The first was the story in the First Book of Samuel, chapter 23, of David's escape from Saul at Keilah. David, having heard that Saul was planning to go to Keilah and destroy the town because of him, asked the oracle of God 'Will Saul come down as your servant has heard?' The oracle replied, 'He will come down.' David then asked, 'Will the chief men of Keilah hand me and my men over to Saul?' The oracle replied, 'They will hand you over.' At the receipt of this information David made off, and thus escaped being handed over to Saul.

The second text came from the Wisdom of Solomon 4:11. This is a description of the premature death of a virtuous man. 'He has been carried off so that evil may not warp his understanding or treachery seduce his soul.' This Molina took as proving that God must have known that if the good man had not been carried off, evil would have warped his understanding.

The third text was a familiar passage from the New Testament: 'Woe to you Bethsaida! For if the miracles done in you had been done in Tyre and Sidon, they would have repented long ago in sackcloth and ashes' (Matt. 11:21).

The text from the Wisdom of Solomon had had a long history in the theodicy of the Fathers. It was used by the Pelagian opponents of St. Augustine's teaching on grace and predestination. Augustine's disciples, Prosper and Hilary, argued that God's predestination could not depend on foreknowledge of sins, because there were children who died unbaptized and thus were unable to reach Heaven; as these had no sins to be foreseen they must have been reprobated by God independently of his foreknowledge. Their Pelagian adversaries replied that God had determined their loss by his foreknowledge of what they would have done had they grown up. Augustine replied that it was a strange sort of fore-knowledge which was foreknowledge of something which was never going to take place (*De Praedestinatione Sanctorum*, 12).

To defend divine knowledge of counterfactuals Suarez argued that Augustine was not denying that God knew what children would have done if they had not died, but merely attacking those who said that God punished people for what they would have done even if they never did it. The Pelagian idea is far from dead. In *New Essays in Philosophical Theology* (1955), Professor Flew has argued, in connection with the problem of evil, that God does not need to allow people to suffer in order to try their patience, since he knows what they would do in any trial without trying them. And one frequently reads letters to *The Times* from social reformers suggesting that instead of waiting to commit to prison people who committed murders we should imprison in advance persons who we knew would commit murders if not imprisoned.

It would commonly be thought nowadays by theologians that the biblical texts quoted by Molina do not prove his case. The passage about Tyre and Sidon is clearly rhetorical. The knowledge of what people would have done if they had not died, as attributed to God by the Wisdom of Solomon, is no more than a knowledge of their characters and dispositions when alive. The oracle con-sulted by David, the ephod, had only two sides to it, probably marked 'yes' and 'no'. Such an apparatus would be incapable of marking the difference between knowledge of counterfactuals and knowledge of the truth-value of material implications. Since the antecedent of David's questions was false, the same answers would have been appropriate in each case.

Catholic theologians contemporary with Molina criticized him on different grounds. The Dominicans, led by Domingo Banez, attacked the Molinist definition of liberty of indifference as being incompatible with divine omnipotence. The definition includes mention of 'all necessary conditions for action'. Do these condi-tions include divine co-operation? If not, then the actions escape the control of God, and he is not omnipotent; if so, then it is no longer true that the creature is genuinely able to act or not to act. The supporters of Banez agreed with the Molinists that God knew counterfactuals, but they said that his knowledge was based on his own infallible decrees, and not a matter of middle knowledge of possible creatures.

The dispute between the Jesuits and Dominicans became quite fierce, especially in Spain at the turn of the sixteenth century. In 1605 it was ended by a decree of Pope Paul V forbidding both sides to call each other heretics and commanding them to refrain from 'sour words showing bitterness of soul'.

In our own time there has been a surprising revival of Molinism, not among theologians but among philosophers. The success of possible-world semantics in modal logic has encouraged some thinkers to use the apparatus of possible worlds to provide a semantics for counterfactuals and a fresh treatment of some metaphysical topics such as the Problem of Evil.

Alvin Plantinga has made use of the apparatus of possible worlds in presenting a modernized version of the Freewill Defence against the charge that the existence of evil in the world is incompatible with its being the work of a good creator (1967, ch. 6; 1974b, ch. 9). An essential step in Plantinga's procedure is to claim that there are possible worlds which even an omnipotent God cannot actualize. Let us take any counterfactual concerning a free (and thus, according to Plantinga, undetermined) human action: for instance

(1) If Judas had been offered only 20 pieces of silver, he would not have betrayed Jesus.

We can always find another counterfactual with the same antecedent but a contradictory consequent: in this case

(2) If Judas had been offered only 20 pieces of silver, he would (still) have betrayed Jesus.

We may reasonably suppose that exactly one of these counterfactuals is true; and whichever one it is, there will be a possible world which God could not have actualized—if (1) is true the unactualizable possible world will be one in which Judas is offered 20 pieces of silver and betrays Jesus; if (2) is true it will be one in which Judas is offered 20 pieces of silver and does not betray

Jesus. The impossibility of actualizing certain possible worlds may be, Plantinga argues, part of the explanation of the evil in the actual world.

By 'possible world' is meant something which corresponds to a complete state-description of the universe: as Plantinga put it in a popular exposition of his views: 'We can think of a possible world as an enormous state of affairs that has other states of affairs as *parts*. A possible world has so many parts, in fact, that for any state of affairs you pick out, either that state of affairs or else its opposite is a part of that possible world. And that is what makes a possible world complete' (Plantinga 1976, 606). Following Robert Stalnaker and David Lewis, Plantinga explains the truth-conditions of counterfactual propositions in terms of comparative similarities between possible worlds. Proposition (1) above, for instance, is true in a given possible world W if and only if W is more similar to some possible world in which Judas is offered 20 pieces of silver and does not betray Jesus than to any possible world in which Judas is offered 20 pieces of silver and does betray Jesus; and it is true in the actual world if and only if the same condition holds good of the actual world.

If the evil in the world is to be shown to be compatible with its having a wise creator, it is essential that God should know all true counterfactuals about the free actions of actual and possible creatures: for on this will depend which possible worlds he can and which he cannot actualize. Plantinga does indeed explicitly claim that God does know these counterfactuals and thus, in effect, possesses middle knowledge. He too illustrates his discussion with a counterfactual about a bribe—but this time a totally fictional one. Curley Smith, a mayor of Boston, has accepted a bribe of $35,000 to drop his opposition to a freeway: in this case we may wonder whether the following is true:

(3) If Curley had been offered $20,000, he would have accepted the bribe.

Plantinga writes:

Suppose we think about a state of affairs that includes Curley's having been offered $20,000, all relevant conditions—Curley's financial situation, his general acquisitive tendencies, his venality—being the same as in fact, in the actual world. Our question is really whether there is something Curley would have done had this state of affairs been actual.

Would an omniscient being know what Curley would have done—would he know, that is, either that Curley would have taken the bribe or that he would have rejected it? The answer, I should think is obvious and affirmative (1974b, 180).

And in general: God can create Curley in various states of affairs that include his being significantly free with respect to some action A. Furthermore, God knows in advance what Curley would do if created and placed in these states of affairs (1974b, 186).

I wish to argue that Plantinga's account of middle knowledge is incoherent, and for reasons of essentially the same kind as those urged by the Dominicans of the sixteenth century in their criticism of Molinism. I do not wish to raise the general question of the success or failure of the Freewill Defence, but only to assess the coherence of the possible-worlds account of divine foreknowledge of human free actions.

Many philosophers are critical of the whole metaphysic of possible worlds. They have queried whether states of affairs can be identified and individuated in the way the theory demands, and whether the notion of a maximal or complete state of affairs is a coherent one. They have been dubious about the possibility of devising any consistent and plausible method of measuring similarities between different possible worlds in the way in which the Lewis–Stalnaker treatment of counterfactuals seems to demand. They have been sceptical of the possibility of identifying individuals occuring in one possible world with individuals occurring in other possible worlds in the way which would be necessary for knowledge about possible worlds to give information about the capacities, characters, choices, conduct, and fate of actually existing persons.

I share all these misgivings, but I shall not attempt to expound the criticisms or drive them home. For even if the modern explorers of possible worlds have a completely satisfying answer to the objections made along these lines, they cannot succeed in accounting for divine foreknowledge of undetermined human actions in terms of divine omniscience in respect of counterfactuals.

First of all, it is clear that mere knowledge of what human beings do in each of the indefinitely many possible worlds in which they figure will not be enough to predict anything at all about any actual human being. A possible world is perhaps least tendentiously thought of as something corresponding to a complete and coherent story of the universe. Part of one such story is contained in the first few chapters of Genesis. In that story, you will remember, the first significant free human actions occur in the sixth verse of the third chapter, where 'when the woman saw that the tree was good for food, and that it was pleasant to the eyes, and a tree to be desired to make one wise, she took of the fruit thereof, and did eat, and gave also unto her husband with her, and he did eat'. This tells of one possible world. Another story, which followed Genesis up to this point, could contain the words 'did not eat' at the two places where this verse contains 'did eat'. That would tell of a different possible world. If God, before creating either Adam and Eve or heaven and earth, is to know whether, if created, they will sin and fall, it is clearly not enough for him to know that in one possible world they eat the fruit, and in another they do not.

Nor will it be enough for God to know which counterfactuals are true in each possible world.[1] This, on Plantinga's account, will merely add knowledge of the relations of similarities between the various possible worlds. In some possible worlds the counterfactual

If Adam had been tempted before Eve, he would not have fallen

will be true and in others it will be false. But prior to any divine decision to create, this will not suffice to indicate whether the counterfactual is *in fact* true, still less what Adam or Eve will do in the actual world.

A determinist, of course, might claim that some apparently coherent stories of the world are not really coherent. If Adam's actions, for instance, are determined by his character and circumstances, then only one of the versions of the Genesis story really describes a possible world. But both Molina and Plantinga pride themselves on their indeterminism. And for an indeterminist, points in any story where a free choice is made are precisely points where the story has two different and equally coherent continuations.

Now of course neither Molina nor Plantinga claims that the mere knowledge of all possible worlds will suffice for foreknowledge of actual action. What must be added is knowledge of which of the

---

[1] There is an ambiguity in the sentence 'Before creation, God knew what each creature would do in each possible world.' The ambiguity is due to the English word 'would' doing duty both as the past tense of 'will' and as the subjunctive. The ambiguity is between the two sentences which before creation would be expressed as follows: 'God knows what each creature *will* do in each possible world', and 'God knows what each creature *would* do in each possible world.'

possible worlds is actual: and this knowledge, for Molina at least, is possessed by God simply in virtue of his own decision to create, to actualize one of the many possible worlds. Now if this decision is to be the basis of God's infallible knowledge of free action God must know, when deciding to create, which possible worlds he can create; and when he actualizes a possible world he must know with certainty which possible world he is actualizing.

But can God really know, on the account given by Molina and Plantinga, which world he is creating, which possible world he is actualizing? There may seem to be no difficulty here: he selects a particular possible world and decides to actualize it or, if you prefer, takes a particular coherent world-history and decides to enact it. But if the world-history in question contains undetermined free human actions, then the matter is not so simple, as Plantinga himself insists. We must distinguish between two senses of 'actualize':

You are free with respect to an action A only if God does not bring it about or cause it to be the case that you refrain from A. But now suppose that God knows that if he creates you free with respect to A in some set S of circumstances, you will refrain from A; suppose further that he brings it about . . . that you *are* free with respect to A in S; and suppose finally that you do in fact freely refrain from A. Then in a broader sense of 'bring about' we could properly say that God has brought it about that you freely refrain from A. We must make a corresponding distinction, then, between a stronger and a weaker sense of 'actualize'. In the strong sense, God can actualize only what he can *cause* to be actual; in that sense he cannot actualize any state of affairs including the existence of creatures who freely take some action or other. (1974b, 172–3)

Even if we take 'actualize' in the weaker sense, it is not the case that God can actualize just any possible world. Let us return again to the venal Curley. Even if God can strongly actualize a world in which Curley is offered a bribe, it does not follow that he can weakly actualize that a world in which Curley accepts a bribe of \$20,000. Whether he can weakly actualize that world depends on what Curley would have done if God had strongly actualized the world in which Curley was offered a bribe of \$20,000:

Accordingly, there are possible worlds such that it is partly up to

Curley whether or not God can actualize them. It is of course up to
God whether or not to create Curley, and also up to God whether
or not to make him free with respect to the action of taking the bribe
at t. But if he creates him, and creates him free with respect to this
action, then whether or not he takes it is up to Curley—not God.
(1974b, 184)

Suppose we restrict ourselves to the consideration of those
worlds which, on Plantinga's account, God *can* weakly actualize.
Even these, it seems, he can only actualize if he knows the relevant
counterfactuals about the behaviour of free humans like Curley in
advance of his decision strongly to actualize those parts of the
possible world that he can directly bring about. ('In advance' here
is not to be taken to denote temporal priority—it refers simply to
a logically prior stage of decision-making.) But prior to God's
decision to actualize a particular world those counterfactuals cannot
yet be known: for their truth-value depends, on Plantinga's own
showing, on which world is the actual world. It is not simply that
God's knowledge of these counterfactuals cannot be *based on* a
decision which has to be taken *subsequent* to knowledge of them:
were that the only problem, a Molinist could retreat to the
position that God's knowledge of the counterfactuals is simply
groundless knowledge for which no explanation is possible or
necessary. (Such seems to have been Suarez's position, and perhaps
it is also Plantinga's.) The problem is that what makes the counterfactuals true is not yet there at any stage at which it is undecided
which world is the actual world. The very truth-conditions which
the possible-world semantics were introduced to supply are absent
under the hypothesis that it is undetermined which world the
actual world is to be. But if the truth-conditions are not fulfilled,
the propositions are not true; and if they are not true not even an
omniscient being can know them.

In advance of the decision to create, then, God cannot know
which of the relevant counterfactuals are true. In the absence of
this knowledge, he cannot know which worlds it is in his power to
actualize; and in the absence of that knowledge in its turn it seems
that his decision to create can hardly be the all-wise one which
Molinists have always claimed it to be.

The very notion of actualization is a suspect one, involving the
dubious elements of the metaphysic of possible worlds. To actualize
a world, on the face of it, is to turn a non-actual world into an

actual one: but a moment's reflection shows this to be a self-contradictory feat which not even omnipotence could achieve. No doubt the Molinist will reply that he does not mean that God turns a non-actual world into an actual one, but that he has from all eternity made actual a world which but for his decision would not have been actual; and that continuously he is making actual particular states of affairs which before his actualization were non-actual states of affairs. But even this formulation presupposes that one and the same individual state of affairs may change from possessing the property of being merely possible to possessing the property of being actual. And this involves the type of identification across possible worlds which is found unintelligible by many critics. Unactual states of affairs can no more be individuated, many philosophers claim, than non-existent persons can: there can be no individuation without actualization.

I believe this objection to be a sound one: but once again my criticism of Molinism does not depend upon it. The difficulty is simply that if it is to be possible for God to know which world he is actualizing, then his middle knowledge must be logically prior to his decision to actualize; whereas if middle knowledge is to have an object, the actualization must already have taken place. As long as it is undetermined which action an individual human being will take, it is undetermined which possible world is the actual world—undetermined not just epistemologically, but metaphysically. And as long as it is undetermined which world is actual, it is undetermined which counterfactuals about human free behaviour are true.

The most sophisticated attempts to reconcile divine foreknowledge with the indeterminacy of human free action thus prove on examination to break down. In the next chapter we shall turn to accounts of divine foreknowledge of men's deeds which reject indeterminism and which rely on the project of reconciling human desert and guilt with the predetermination of human conduct.

VI. FOREKNOWLEDGE AND DETERMINISM

Among the theses which Luther nailed to the door at Wittenberg in 1517 was one attacking the freedom of the will. Pope Leo X, in his Bull *Exsurge Domine* condemning Luther in 1519, anathematized the proposition: 'freewill after sin is merely an empty title'. A number of Catholic writers took up the pen against Luther's attack on free will, including More, Fisher, Erasmus, and King Henry VIII. The high point of the ensuing debate was Erasmus's *Diatribe de Libero Arbitrio* (1524) and Luther's *De Servo Arbitrio* (1525).

Erasmus argues for free will principally from the Old and New Testaments and from the authority of the church: philosophically he is unsubtle.[1] Divine foreknowledge, he says, does not cause what is to take place: even we humans know many things which will happen in the future. These things will not happen because we know them; we know them because they will happen. An eclipse of the sun does not occur because astronomers predict it: it can be predicted precisely because it is going to take place. Clearly, this will not do as a defence of free will. Astronomers can predict eclipses because of the necessity of the laws of celestial mechanics; a theory of free will which left us no freer than the stars in their courses reconciles divine foreknowledge with freedom only by evacuating freedom.

Erasmus tries to avoid philosophical complications: it is a piece of irreligious curiosity to ask whether it is correct to say (as Scotus and other scholastics said) that God's foreknowledge is a contingent matter. Luther, though no friend to the scholastics, is enraged by this. 'If this is irreligious, curious, and superfluous,' he asks,

---

[1] Both Erasmus and Luther claim the authority of Lorenzo Valla's *Dialogue on Free Will*. This lively dialogue mainly covers ground familiar from ancient and medieval authors: but it adds a distinction between the foreseeability and predictability of human actions. Foresight may be possible when prediction is not. Suppose that I know you are so countersuggestible that you will do the opposite of what I foretell. I offer to foretell which foot you will move next, and predict that you will move the right foot. As I foresaw, but could not foretell to you, you then move the left foot.

'what, then, is religious serious and useful knowledge?' 'This is weak stuff, Erasmus,' he goes on, '*Das ist zu viel*', breaking into German in the middle of his Latin text (WA 610). For Luther himself, God foresees nothing contingently. 'He foresees, purposes and does all things according to His immutable, eternal and infallible will. This thunderbolt throws free will flat and utterly dashes it to pieces' (WA 615). Does this mean, as Erasmus had claimed, that Luther's teaching is the same as that of Wycliff condemned at the Council of Constance, that everything we do happens not on account of our free will, but out of sheer necessity? In reply, Luther distinguishes between senses of 'necessity':

By necessity I do not mean compulsion. I mean what they term the necessity of immutability. That is to say, a man void of the Spirit of God does not do evil against his will . . . he does it spontaneously and willingly.

On the other hand, when God works in us the will . . . desires and acts not from compulsion, but responsively of its own desire and inclination.

The human will is like a beast of burden: if God rides it it wills and goes where God wills; if Satan rides it it wills and goes where Satan wills. It must go where its rider bids, and it is not free to choose its rider (WA 634–5).

Luther prefers to drop altogether the term 'free will'; but the spontaneity which he here allows to human action has been regarded by many subsequent philosophers and theologians as being the only thing which can genuinely be meant by the term. Freedom so understood ('liberty of spontaneity') has been contrasted with the type of ability to do otherwise ('liberty of indifference') which for Scotus and Molina and many more recent thinkers constituted the essence of human freedom.

For Luther, both good men and bad men do what they want: what they lack is the ability to change their desires (this is the 'necessity of immutability'): the will is not free, in the sense that it cannot change itself from a bad will into a good one; it can only passively undergo such a change at the hand of God. Spontaneity, understood as lack of compulsion, is something which is compatible with determinism; and Luther argues in favour of determinism by appealing to divine foreknowledge:[1]

[1] It is a matter of dispute among commentators how universally Luther

If God foreknew that Judas would be a traitor, Judas became a traitor of necessity, and it was not in the power of Judas, nor of any creature, to alter it, or change his will from that which God has foreseen. . . . If God be not deceived in that which he foreknows, then that which He foreknows must of necessity come to pass. Otherwise, who could believe His promises, who would fear His threatenings if what He promised or threatened did not necessarily ensue?' (WA, 715–16)

Luther knows that scholastics distinguished between the necessity of the consequence ('Necessarily, if God knows that p, then p') and the necessity of the consequent ('If God knows that p, then necessarily p'). But, he says, nothing has been achieved by these means beyond imposing upon the unlearned.[1]

Thomas More, in his *Dialogue against Tyndale*, sums up Luther's teaching thus:

Item he teacheth that no man hath no fre wyll, nor can any thyng do therein . . . every thinge that we do good and bad we do nothing at all there in our self but only suffer God to do all thing in us good and badde, as wax is wrought into an ymage or a candel by the mans hand without anything doyng thereto itself.

To counter this, More asks what would be the use of reason to man:

if man hath no power of himself toward the direction of his own works, but that all our works were brought forth of us without our will, worse than the works be, indeed, out of a brute beast by the appetite of his sensual motion? For ours should be by this spirit brought forth, as the leaves come out of the tree, or as a stone falleth downward and the smoke upward, by the force of nature. (More, 1931, 196)

More exaggerates Luther's position: the wax does not consent to become a candle, as Luther's sinner consents to his sin. Even on Luther's account there is a great difference between an external force acting on an irrational object, and the force of desire working

---

extended his determinism. According to Urban, 1971, Luther was a thorough-going determinist, and the first theologian explicitly to offer a proof of determinism from divine foreknowledge; all earlier theologians, he claims, thought with Aquinas that the deterministic inference could be blocked.

[1] The distinction is a genuine and important one. But since, as the scholastics —correctly—accepted, whatever is necessarily implied by a necessary proposition is itself necessary, if God's knowledge is itself necessary (as Luther believed) then it follows that the consequent is necessary also, and so the distinction does not suffice to reconcile foreknowledge with contingency.

within a human being. But More tells an anecdote which raises a more interesting issue:

One of their sect was served in a good turn in Almayne, which when he had robbed a man and was brought before the judges, he would not deny the deed, but said it was his destiny to do it, and therefore they might not blame him; they answered him, after his own doctrines, that if it were his destiny to steal and that therefore they must hold him excused, then it was also their destiny to hang him, and therefore he must as well hold them excused again.

The twist in the story is a very old one, going back to the Stoic Zeno (see Diogenes Laertius, VII, 23):[1] the implicit argument is valid against anyone seeking to excuse himself for a misdeed on the grounds that (1) determinism is true and (2) if determinism is true everything is excusable. But though Luther held the first premiss, he would surely have rejected the second, since he believed that God justly punished sinners who could not do otherwise than sin. But whether or not he was fair to Luther, More's anecdote points to the major difficulty facing anyone who claims that human beings have no freedom other than spontaneity. How is the mere presence of spontaneity in human action (whether or not it is called 'free will') sufficient to justify holding human beings responsible and punishable for their deeds? From Luther's time to our own, this question has consistently been put by defenders of liberty of indifference to defenders of liberty of spontaneity.

Luther's doctrine of the enslaved will was condemned at the Council of Trent. Thenceforth all Catholic writers defended some form of freedom of the will: but by no means all of them defended the theory of liberty of indifference as propounded by Jesuits such as Suarez and Molina. Dominican writers such as Domingo Bañez, like Luther, explained human action in terms of spontaneity; unlike Luther they tried to show that human actions were contingent and free despite antecedent divine causality. The Oratorian Father Gibieuf, in his *De Libertate Dei et Creaturae*, attacked the Jesuit definition of liberty in terms of an absolute indifference to act or not to act. If this is what liberty consists in, Gibieuf argued, then a man never acts less freely than when he acts freely. For when a man acts, he is not indifferent with regard to acting, but is determined by his very act. To say that it is enough

[1] I am indebted to Mr M. Reeves for this reference.

that he had the power not to act at the time when he was on the point of acting, Gibieuf argued, is to say that liberty is only for future actions qua future.

An argument of this kind, as we saw in the preceding chapter, had been countered in advance by Molina in his discussion of Ockham. Gibieuf's claim trades on an equivocation in the word 'determine', which may mean 'necessitate' and may mean 'settle for certain'. The two senses are quite different, one being metaphysical and the other epistemological. The difference between the two is most clearly seen with regard to the past: my researches may determine the causes of the Thirty Years War—i.e. settle for certain what they were—without in any way necessitating or bringing about the war. When I act, by acting I settle for certain what it is that I am doing; I do not, however, by acting *necessitate* my own action, or affect what I *can* do in the sense of what powers I have. Confused though it is, Gibieuf's argument later became a regular weapon in the arsenal of anti-Molinist criticism.

Gibieuf's own account of free will was the rather implausible theory that a human being was free if and only if he was acting for the sake of the supreme good. The principal importance of his opinions in the history of philosophy was the influence which they exercised on his admirer Descartes.

Descartes's own position, like Gibieuf's, was closer to that of the Dominicans than of the Jesuits. 'Freewill', he wrote in the *Fourth Meditation*, 'consists simply in the fact that we are able alike to do and not to do a given thing (that is, can either assert or deny, either seek or shun); or rather, simply in the fact that our impulse towards what our intellect presents to us as worthy of assertion, or denial, as a thing to be sought or shunned, is such that we feel ourselves not to be determined by any external force' (AT VII, 57; HR I, 175). The Seventh Axiom in the axiomatic presentation of his system in the *Second Replies* reads, 'The will of a thinking thing is impelled, voluntarily of course and freely, since that is of the essence of the will, but none the less infallibly, towards a good clearly known to it' (AT VII, 166; HR II, 56).

These definitions clearly place the essence of freedom in liberty of spontaneity. Descartes did think that there was such a thing as liberty of indifference, but it was possible only in the absence of clear and distinct perception: once one clearly and distinctly perceived a good, one was impelled towards it. Liberty of indifference could occur where the reasons pro and con a course of action were equally balanced; or where a perverted will chose what it (obscurely) knew to be the worse course.

Oddly enough, when Descartes actually comes to explain the relationship between divine foreknowledge and human freedom, he does so in ways which are much more appropriate to a Molinist account of the matter than to a Bañezian one. In a letter to Princess Elizabeth of January 1646, he wrote:

I turn to your Highness' problem about free will. I will try to give an illustration to explain how this is both dependent and free. Suppose that a King has forbidden duels, and knows with certainty that two gentlemen of his kingdom who live in different towns have a quarrel, and are so hostile to each other that if they meet nothing will stop them from fighting. If this King orders one of them to go on a certain day to the town where the other lives, and orders the other to go on the same day to the place where the first is, he knows with certainty that they will meet, and fight, and thus disobey his prohibition; but none the less he does not compel them, and his knowledge, and even his will to make them act thus, does not prevent their combat when they meet being as voluntary and as free as if they had met on some other occasion and he had known nothing about it. And they can be no less justly punished for disobeying the prohibition.

Now what a King can do in such a case, concerning certain free actions of his subjects, God, with His infinite foresight and power does infallibly in regard to all the free actions of all men. Before He sent us into the world He knew exactly what all the inclinations of our will would be; it is He who gave us them, it is He who has disposed all the other things outside us so that such and such objects would present themselves to our senses at such and such times, on the occasion of which he knew that our freewill would determine us to such and such an action; and He so willed, but without using any compulsion. In the King of my story it is possible to distinguish two different types of volition, one according to which he willed that these gentlemen should fight, since he caused them to meet; and the other according to which he willed that they should not, since he forbade duels. In the same way the theologians make a distinction in God's willing: He has an absolute and independent will, according to which He wills all things to come about as they do, and another relative will which concerns the merit and demerit of men, according to which he wants them to obey his laws. (K, 188)

Some historians of philosophy have found this passage inconsistent with Descartes's theory of the will: but with benign inter-

pretation it can perhaps be made coherent with it. Descartes is
not saying, as a Molinist would, that God knows, before he sends
us into the world, what our actions will be, because he has already
seen what we would do in all possible worlds: he says that God
knows what we will do because he knows what *he* will do in the
actual world. Since, on Descartes's theory, our perceptions of
goodness determine our actions without depriving them of freedom,
God can control and therefore predict our free actions by arranging
our perceptions.

It remains difficult, however, to see how Descartes is to account
for divine foreknowledge of actions in situations where the
prospects of good and evil appear evenly matched. He seems to
allow the possibility of such cases of indifference: cases where the
will is not inclined so much in a single direction as to rule out the
possibility of it acting in the opposite direction. His parable
of the malignant duellists suggests no account of divine foreknowledge in such cases; and yet it is only in such cases that the actions
of human beings seem to be genuinely contingent.

Moreover, Descartes is profoundly mistaken to argue that what
a King can do in a case like that of the duellists God can do with
regard to all the free actions of all men. It is only because all the
other actions of the duellists that have formed their characters are
independent of the King's desires and control that he can plausibly
be said not to be responsible for their final duel and to be entitled
to punish them for disobeying his prohibition. But on Descartes's
view every free action of every human being is stage-managed by
God just as much as the final act in the duellists' drama. This
destroys the plausibility of the parallel.

Descartes was a Catholic living in a Protestant country: a fact
which may partially explain the ambiguities of his position.
But by the time he wrote Catholics and Protestants were not
simply lined up for or against free will as in the days of More
and Luther. The Reformer Melanchthon modified Luther's
position in the direction of freedom, and free will is not denied in
the Augsburg confession which set the standard for Lutheran
churches. For Calvin, though all creatures are necessitated instru-
ments of God's will, the necessity imposed on creatures involves
no compulsion on free creatures. A doctrine of free will very close
to that of the Jesuits was defended in the Reformed church at the
turn of the sixteenth century by Arminius, a divine of the University

of Leyden. Arminian views found favour in the Church of England, as Hobbes was later to complain:

For some ages past, the doctors of the Roman church have exempted from the dominion of God's will the will of man; and brought in a doctrine, that not only man, but also his will is free, and determined to this or that action, not by the will of God, nor necessary causes, but by the power of the will itself. And though by the reformed Churches instructed by Luther, Calvin and others, this opinion was cast out, yet not many years since it began again to be reduced by Arminius and his followers, and became the readiest way to ecclesiastical promotion. (Morgenbesser and Walsh, 1962, 41)

The dispute between Arminians and strict Calvinists concerned not only divine foreknowledge of human action but also, and principally, the nature of the decrees of the divine will which predestined those who were to be saved and reprobated those who were to be damned. The Arminian Remonstrants of Gouda affirmed that the divine decrees were not absolute, but conditional upon the exercise of human freedom; that God's foreknowledge was logically prior to the decisions of his will and was not based upon them; and that he merely foresaw and did not necessitate future contingent events. Among Dutch Calvinists the stricter party prevailed at the Synod of Dort in 1619, which reaffirmed the unconditioned nature of divine election.[1] The dispute, as I have said, principally concerned the divine will, not divine foreknowledge; but of course the distinction between the two is itself one of the points at issue. Within a deterministic framework one cannot draw the same sharp distinction between those things which God directly wills, and those which he merely foresees and permits, which is insisted on by indeterminists whether Jesuit or Arminian.

An elegant, though no doubt untypical, exposition of an Arminian position is to be found in John Milton's *De Doctrina Christiana* (Milton, 1933). In the third chapter of the work ('Of the

---

[1] There was a further division among the stricter Calvinists about the order of the divine decrees. Infralapsarians held that the divine decree to save part and to damn part of the human race was subsequent to the decree that Adam should fall; supralapsarians held that the fall of Adam was chosen as a means to the salvation of some and damnation of others. The dispute did not concern a temporal sequence of decisions; the point at issue was which events in the history of humankind figured in God's plan as means and which as ends. All the events were objects of divine will and not mere permission or prescience. See Prior, 1957, 20.

divine decrees') Milton argues that no divine decrees concerning things which are within the power of free agents can be understood as absolute decrees: they always have tacit or explicit conditions. He argues for this by citing unfulfilled predictions and threats from the Bible, and by claiming that the doctrine of absolute divine decrees would take away from human affairs all liberty of action and all endeavour and desire to do right.

For we might argue thus: If God have at all events decreed my salvation, however I may act, I shall not perish. 'But God has also decreed as the means of your salvation that you should act rightly.' I cannot, therefore, but act rightly at some time or other, since God has so decreed; in the mean time I will do as I please; if I never act rightly, it will be seen that I was never predestinated to salvation, and that whatever good I might have done would have been to no purpose. (Milton, 1933, 71)

Like More's argument against Luther this objection to determinism recurs often in the history of philosophy. Unlike More's argument, it is not valid. Consider the propositions:

(1) If I act rightly, I will be saved
(2) If I do not act rightly, I will be saved.

If I am predestined, then the consequent of each of these propositions is true; and if we interpret each of the propositions as truth-functional conditionals, each of them will on that supposition be true; in that sense, as Milton says, 'however I may act, I shall not perish'. But if the propositions are to be useful in deliberating how to behave, they must be understood not simply truth-functionally, but also as supporting the corresponding counterfactuals:

(1') If I acted rightly, I would be saved
(2') If I did not act rightly, I would be saved.

But (2) understood truth-functionally may be true without (2')'s being true. Similarly, the following proposition, taken truth-functionally, may be true:

(3) If I do good I will be damned

while the following is false:

(3') If I did good I would be damned.

But only if (3′) is true is Milton justified in saying 'whatever good I might have done would have been to no purpose'.

Milton rejects the Calvinist distinction between the necessity of compulsion and the necessity of immutability. Any kind of necessary connection between divine decrees and human actions, he argues, would make God responsible for men's sins:

Divine necessity, they say, imposes no constraint upon the liberty of free agents. I answer, if it do not constrain, it either determines, or co-operates, or is wholly inactive. If it determine or co-operate, it is either the sole or the joint and principal cause of every action, whether good or bad, of free agents. If it be wholly inactive, it cannot be called a cause in any sense, much less can it be termed necessity. (Milton, 1933, 33)

God's decrees concerning human beings are of conditional form, with the antecedents describing free human actions. Thus: 'If thou eat not the forbidden fruit, thou shalt live; if thou eat, thou shalt die.'

So understood, the divine decrees appear to be neither decisions nor predictions, but rather commands with sanctions attached. As such, they seem quite inadequate to be an expression of any infallible divine foreknowledge of human actions. Milton tries to avoid this:

Future events which God has foreseen, will happen certainly, but not of necessity. They will happen certainly, because the divine prescience cannot be deceived, but they will not happen necessarily, because prescience can have no influence on the object foreknown. . . . What therefore is to happen according to contingency and the free will of man, is not the effect of God's prescience, but is produced by the free agency of its own natural causes, the future spontaneous inclination of which is perfectly known to God. Thus God foreknew that Adam would fall of his own free will; his fall was therefore certain, but not necessary, since it proceeded from his own free will, which is incompatible with necessity. (Milton, 1933, 87)

Milton does not explain how this certain knowledge is possible in the absence of necessity. Were he to try to give an account, it seems that he would have to appeal—as many Arminians did— to something very like the Molinist doctrine of middle knowledge; and this solution, as we have seen, is untenable.

A defender of Milton's Arminian position might say that no

account could, or should, be given of *how* God knows the future: we must simply assert *that* he knows and not expect to be able to shed any light on the mysterious and unique nature of his knowledge. The most that a theist can be called upon to do is to demonstrate that foreknowledge of an undetermined future does not involve a flat contradiction; and this much is achieved by Milton's distinction between certainty and necessity. To attempt to do more is to invite upon ourselves the fate of the devils in *Paradise Lost* who sat in Hell:

>   and reason'd high
> Of Providence, Foreknowledge, Will, and Fate,
> Fixt Fate, free will, foreknowledge absolute,
> And found no end, in wand'ring mazes lost.   (II, 558–61)

But the certain foreknowledge which Milton attributes to God is not, in fact, consistent with a genuine lack of necessity in future events. This was shown conclusively by the eighteenth-century American Calvinist theologian Jonathan Edwards, in the chapter of his book *On the Freedom of the Will* which bears the heading 'God's certain Foreknowledge of the future volitions of moral agents, inconsistent with such a Contingence of those volitions as is without all necessity'. Edwards argues thus:

To say that God certainly, and without all conjecture, knows that a thing will infallibly be, which at the same time he knows to be so contingent, that it may possibly not be, is to suppose his knowledge inconsistent with itself; or that one thing that he knows is utterly inconsistent with another thing that he knows. Tis the same thing as to say, he now knows a proposition to be of certain infallible truth, which he knows to be of contingent uncertain truth. If a future volition is so without all necessity, that there is nothing hinders but that it may not be, then the proposition which asserts its future existence, is so uncertain, that there is nothing hinders but that the truth of it may entirely fail. And if God knows all things, he knows this proposition to be thus uncertain. And that is inconsistent with his knowing that it is infallibly true; and so inconsistent with his infallibly knowing that it is true. If the thing be indeed contingent, God views it so, and judges it to be contingent if he views things as they are. If the event be not necessary, then it is possible it may never be: and if it be possible it may never be, God knows it may possibly never be; and that is to know that the proposition which affirms its existence, may possibly not be true; and that is to know that the truth of it is uncertain, which surely is inconsistent with his knowing it as a certain truth. (Edwards, 1959, 260–1)

Edwards's attack on the attempt to reconcile contingency with certain foreknowledge seems to me entirely successful: but his further criticism of the notion of liberty of indifference is less well inspired. The notion is an incoherent one, he argues, because

choice and preference can no more be in a state of indifference than motion can be in a state of rest, or than the preponderance of the scale of a balance can be in a state of equilibrium. Motion may be the next moment after rest; but can't exist with it, in *any*, even the *least* part of it. So choice may be immediately after a state of indifference, but has no coexistence with it: even the very beginning of it is not in a state of indifference. And therefore if this be liberty no act of the will in any degree is ever performed in a state of liberty. (Edwards, 1959, 261)

Now whatever Edwards's Arminian contemporaries may have meant by 'indifference', the Jesuit theologians who first fully worked out the theory of liberty of indifference did not mean by the word a state of equal inclination towards each of a pair of alternative options. If an agent does X in a state of liberty of indifference that, for Molina, meant simply that he did X while having the power and opportunity not to do X; and having that power and opportunity is perfectly compatible with having a strong inclination or desire to do X and no inclination at all not to do X. Edwards's criticism then, however much it may have told against his immediate Arminian opponents, does not in any way disable the theory of liberty of indifference in itself.

Edwards himself defines freedom as liberty of spontaneity: liberty is 'the power, opportunity, or advantage that any one has to do as he pleases'; the power to conduct oneself according to one's pleasure, irrespective of how one's pleasure comes to be as it is. His positive account depends heavily on a naïve theory of mental causation: he thinks of pleasure or choice as a mental event which causes action, and as being itself causally necessitated (by a mysterious method of necessitation which he calls moral, as opposed to physical, necessitation) by the motives presented to the agent. He can thus claim that human beings act freely (because they act in accordance with their choice) and yet necessarily (because their choices are determined by a series of causes going back to the first cause). He thus makes his own a distinction between freedom to act and freedom to will which was adumbrated by Luther and clearly stated by Hobbes. Writing of his Arminian adversary Bishop Bramhall of Derry, Hobbes says:

I did let him know a man was free, in those things that were in his power, to follow his will; but that he was not free to will, that is, that his will did not follow his will. Which I expressed in these words. 'The question is whether the will to write, or the will to forbear, come upon a man according to his will, or according to anything else in his own power.' He that cannot understand the difference between *free to do it if he will* and *free to will* is not fit . . . to hear this controversy disputed, much less to be a writer in it. (Morgenbesser and Walsh, 1962, 48)

Because Edwards, like Hobbes, conceived of willing as a mental event antecedent to and distinct from acting, he can threaten Arminian defenders of freedom of the will with a vicious regress:

The meaning [of the Arminians] must be that a man has power to will as he pleases or chooses to will: that is, he has power by one act of choice, to choose another; by an antecedent act of will to choose a consequent act; and therein to execute his own choice. And if this be their meaning, it is nothing but shuffling with those they dispute with, and baffling their own reason. For still the question returns, wherein lies man's liberty in that antecedent of will which chose the consequent act? The answer according to the same principles must be, that his liberty in this also lies in his willing as he would, or as he chose, or agreeable to another act of choice preceding that. And so the question returns in infinitum, and the like answer must be made in infinitum: in order to support their opinion there must be no beginning, but free acts of will must have been chosen by foregoing free acts of will, in the soul of every man, without beginning; and so before he had a being, from all eternity. (Edwards, 1959, 193)

Edwards's argument is valid, and has been used in our own time by Gilbert Ryle, against the theory that what makes an action's voluntary is its being preceded and caused by an independently identifiable mental event such as an act of choice or volition. If volitions are involuntary, they cannot give rise to voluntary action; if they are voluntary, then according to the theory they must themselves be preceded by other volitions and so *ad infinitum*. But the theory of causally effective volitions is no necessary part of the notion of liberty of indifference. According to the partisans of liberty of indifference, what makes an action's voluntary is not its being preceded by a special kind of event; it is its being performed by an agent possessing the power to act differently: the possession of a power is not a mental event and not a causally operative agent. The distinction between the freedom to act and the freedom to will which Hobbes considered a prerequisite for the discussion of the freedom of the will in fact involves a tendentious parallelism between willing and doing which fatally obscures the issue. The will is simply the ability to act freely; and the exercise of the will is the free action itself.

The work of philosophers such as Ryle and Wittgenstein in the present century has shown that the mental mechanisms which were postulated by seventeeth- and eighteenth-century determinists are entirely mythical entities. But this does not destroy the interest of the attempts of Hobbes and Edwards to reconcile determinism with freedom. For while psychological determinism may be incoherent, there may be other coherent forms of determinism: neurophysiological determinism for instance. One may accept that there is a profound misunderstanding involved in the idea that a man's actions may be determined by his wants and intentions, and yet be willing to entertain the possibility that his behaviour is capable of deterministic explanation in terms of neurophysiological states and processes.

Freedom is indeed, I believe, compatible with determinism, as Edwards maintained. I have argued this at length elsewhere (Kenny, 1976, 145–61; 1978, 30–3); here I can only baldly summarize the argument. The partisans of liberty of indifference were indeed right to insist that there can only be genuine freedom where there is the power of alternative action. But this power can be present even in cases where it is predetermined that it will not be exercised. The power to perform an action involves both ability and opportunity. I may possess an ability to X even at times when I am not X-ing: the test of whether I have an ability is whether, if I wanted to X and there was an opportunity to X, I would succeed in X-ing. Equally, I may possess an opportunity to X without making use of that opportunity by X-ing: I possess such an opportunity provided that nothing independent of my own wants prevents me from X-ing. Therefore the possession of both an ability and opportunity to X need not be ruled out by its being determined (say by physiological laws) that I will not X: it will not be ruled out provided that the physiological state which I am in and which determines my not X-ing is one which I would not be in if I wanted to X. Thus the possibility of acting freely—of acting while possessing the ability and opportunity to act otherwise—is not ruled out by physiological determinism.

I do not wish to maintain that physiological determinism is true: I know of no convincing reason to believe that it is true or to believe that it is false. But it is clear that if it is true—if human actions are identifiable with pieces of physiologically determined behaviour—then the problem of divine foreknowledge of human action is very much simplified. Assuming that not only are human actions determined by human physiology, but that the physiological laws themselves form part of a total system of deterministic laws governing the whole universe, God can predict what each human being will do simply in virtue of knowing the initial conditions and the deterministic laws which he has himself imposed on the world he created. And if the determinism is compatible with freedom, then there will be no reason why the future human actions may not be genuinely free (though, as Luther and Edwards insisted against Scotus and Ockham, the propositions predicting them will be necessary rather than contingent).

Such a system will, then, account for divine foreknowledge; but it can scarcely escape the difficulty, on which Milton insisted, that it makes God responsible for human misdeeds. Calvinist writers, from Calvin himself onwards, have insisted that a man's being determined to act need not necessarily exempt him from moral responsibility for his actions. Anyone who accepts the compatibility of determinism with freedom must agree that agents can be justly blamed and punished for acts which they were predetermined to perform, provided only they had the ability and opportunity to refrain from them. But if the Calvinist system is to be tenable, it must be possible to show not only that human beings can be involved in blame for determined sins, but that God can avoid responsibility for them. And this seems to be much more difficult to show. For if an agent freely and knowingly sets in motion a deterministic process with a certain upshot, it seems that he must be responsible for that upshot. Calvin argued rightly that the truth of determinism would not make everything that happens in the world happen by God's intention: only some of the events of history would be chosen by God as ends or means, others could be merely consequences of his choices. But that would not suffice to acquit God of responsibility for sin. For moral agents are responsible not only for their intentional actions, but also for the consequences of their actions: for states of affairs which they bring about voluntarily but not intentionally. An indeterminist can make a distinction between those states of affairs which God causes, and those which he merely permits: but in a deterministic created universe the distinction between causing and permitting would have no application to God.

Whether determinism is true or false, therefore, it seems that there cannot be a God who infallibly knows future free actions, and yet is not the author of sin. If determinism is true, it is comparatively easy to explain how he can infallibly foresee free action, but impossibly difficult to show how he is not the author of sin. If indeterminism is true, the Freewill Defence can be offered to exonerate God for responsibility for sin, but no coherent account seems possible of his infallible knowledge of future free actions.

PART THREE

OMNIPOTENCE

VII. THE DEFINITION OF OMNIPOTENCE

It is by no means easy to state concisely and coherently what is meant by 'omnipotence'. Omniscience appears to be analogous to omnipotence: just as omniscience is knowing everything, so omnipotence is being able to do everything. But whereas it is easy to define what it is to be omniscient, it is not so easy to define omnipotence. A being X is omniscient iff, for all p, if p, then X knows that p. We cannot offer a simply parallel definition of omnipotence: X is omnipotent iff, for all p, if p, then X can bring it about that p. For this, though it would attribute considerable power to X, would not attribute to him power to do anything which has not already been done, or will not sometime be done. On the other hand, if we drop the if-clause, and say that X is omnipotent iff for all p, X can bring it about that p, then we attribute to X a power far beyond what has traditionally been ascribed to God. For, with the possible exception of Descartes, no theologian or philosopher has seriously maintained that God can bring it about that contradictories are true together. But if, for all p, God can bring it about that p, then, by substitution we can conclude that he can bring it about that both p and not p; that mice are both larger and smaller than elephants, or what you will. Nor can one say that, for all ϕ, God can ϕ; for it seems clear that there will be some substitutions for 'ϕ' which will not give truths when applied to God, such as 'cough', 'sin', or 'die'.

Aquinas rehearses some of the difficulties about omnipotence in the seventh article of the first question of the *De Potentia*. He concludes that God cannot be said to be omnipotent in the sense of being simply able to do everything (*quia omnia possit absolute*). He considers a number of other suggestions. One, attributed to St. Augustine, is that God is omnipotent in the sense that he can do whatever he wants to do. But to this there are serious objections. The blessed in heaven, St. Thomas says, and perhaps even the happy on earth, can do whatever they want; otherwise there would be something lacking in their happiness. But they are not called omnipotent. So it is not enough for the omnipotence which is a divine attribute that God should be able to do whatever he wants. Indeed, a wise man restricts his wants to what is within his power. If he succeeds in this degree of self-control, it will be true of him that he can do whatever he wants. But it is not true that every wise man is an omnipotent man.

Aquinas turns to the formulation: God can do whatever is possible. He raises the question: what does 'possible' mean here? Does it mean: whatever is naturally possible, or whatever is supernaturally possible, i.e. possible to God? If the former, then divine omnipotence does not exceed the power of nature and is no great thing. If the latter, then to say that God is omnipotent is a tautology and the analysis a circumlocution: to say that God is omnipotent is merely to say that God can do all that God can do. And once again, in this sense one can claim that everyone is as omnipotent as God: for everyone can do what he can do.

Aquinas's own account is tantamount to the proposal that the omnipotence of God is the ability to do whatever is logically possible. 'We are left with the alternative', he wrote in the *Summa Theologiae*, 'that he is omnipotent because he can do everything that is absolutely possible.' This possibility is absolute possibility in contrast to the relative possibility just discussed which was possibility relative to a particular agent's powers. 'Something is judged to be possible or impossible from the relationship between its terms: possible when the predicate is compatible with the subject, as, for Socrates to sit; impossible when it is not compatible, as for a man to be a donkey.'

St. Thomas offers a rather dubious reason for this, saying that as God is pure being, not being of any particular kind, anything which qualifies as being (*habet rationem entis*) is a fit object of God's action. He goes on:

Whatever implies being and not being simultaneously is incompatible with the absolute possibility which falls under the divine omnipotence. Such a contradiction is not subject to it, not from any impotence in God, but because it simply does not have the nature of being feasible or possible. Whatever, then, does not involve a contradiction is in that realm of the possible with respect to which God is called omnipotent. Whatever involves a contradiction is not within the scope of omnipotence because it cannot qualify for possibility. Better, however, to say that it cannot be done, rather than that God cannot do it. (*S.Th.* Ia. 25, 3)

Aquinas's solution, however, does not solve the difficulties. We cannot define omnipotence by saying 'For all p, if it is logically possible that p, then God can bring it about that p.' For there are many counter-examples to this which St. Thomas would himself have admitted as counter-examples. For instance, it is no doubt logically possible that Troy did not fall, but according to the common view God cannot (now at any rate) bring it about that Troy did not fall. Moreover, by itself Aquinas's formula does not show us how to deal with a number of familiar puzzles about the idea of omnipotence. It does not show us, for instance, how to answer such questions as 'Can God make an object too heavy for him to lift?' 'Has God the power to make an immovable lamp-post and the power to make an irresistible cannonball?'

St. Thomas does indeed mention some difficulties of this kind; but before considering them it is worth noting that he seems to prefer the formulation 'God's power is infinite' to the formulation 'God is omnipotent.' I shall later argue that this is a sound instinct. However, St. Thomas's argument to this effect is unconvincing. God's active power, he says, is in proportion to his actual being; his actual being is infinite; therefore his active power is infinite. Or, in slightly different terms: The more perfect an agent's form, the more powerful it is (e.g. the hotter something is, the better it can heat); therefore, since God's form or essence is infinite so is his power.

The sense in which God's being is infinite is, however, obscure. From time to time St. Thomas explains it along the following lines: while I am a man and this is a table, there are all kinds of things which I am not and which this table is not; e.g. I am not a horse and this table is not a chair. In the case of God, however, he just *is* and his being is not limited by having any cramping predicates stuck on after the copula. Or, as he puts it in the present article, 'God's being is infinite in so far as it is not limited by any container (*recipiens*).' *Esse* appears to be pictured as a sort of fluid which is boundless in itself and is given form and boundaries by being poured into a particular object as into a bucket. In reading Aquinas on Being, one is constantly torn between considering *esse* in terms of vivid but inapplicable metaphors, and abstract but ill-formed formulas. (See Kenny, 1969b, 70 ff.)

Among the difficulties which Aquinas raises for his account of omnipotence, however, there is one which deserves to be pondered:

'Every power is manifested by its effects; otherwise it would be a vain power. So if God's power were infinite he could produce an infinite effect.' In the *Summa* the answer is given that God is not a univocal agent (i.e. not an agent whose effect is something of the same kind as itself). A human begetter, being an univocal agent, cannot do anything more than breed men, so that the whole of its power is manifested in its effect. The case is different with analogous agents like God and (in Aristotelian cosmology) the sun. The *De Potentia* gives an alternative answer; the very notion of *being made* or *being an effect* is incompatible with infinity because whatever is made from nothing has some defect. Hence the notion of an infinite effect is incoherent. But might one not go on to conclude that the notion of an infinite power is no less incoherent than the notion of an infinite effect?

Aquinas's objection is an ancestor of a number of modern difficulties. We may consider an instructive question posed by John Mackie in his article 'Evil and Omnipotence':

Can an omnipotent being make things which he cannot control? It is clear that this is a paradox; the question cannot be answered satisfactorily either in the affirmative or in the negative. If we answer 'Yes' it follows that if God actually makes things which he cannot control, he is not omnipotent once he has made them: there are then things which he cannot do. But if we answer 'No' we are immediately asserting that there are things which he cannot do, that is to say that he is already not omnipotent. (Mackie, 1955, 210)

It is, I think, clear that the answer to Mackie's question is 'No, he cannot': the problem is to show how this answer is not incompatible with omnipotence.

This cannot be done simply by appeal to the notion of logical impossibility: for whether 'There exists a being whom an omnipotent God cannot control' is a logically possible state of affairs or not depends on what definition we give of omnipotence, and whether the concept is a coherent one.

On the other hand, it seems that we can reverse Mackie's dilemma and ask: Does it make sense to say 'X is a being which even an omnipotent being cannot control'? If it does, then God can make such a being without any loss to his omnipotence, since the ascribing of sense to the formula, however it is done, will have shown that failure to control X is not incompatible with omnipotence. If it does not, then it is no limitation on God's omnipotence to say that God cannot bring it about that such a being exists.

Of course 'X makes a being which X cannot control' is not an impossible sentence-frame; but that does not mean that it will give a possibility with every substitution for 'X', especially if we allow as substitutions phrases like 'a being which can control everything'. Similarly, the fact that both 'X shaves Y' and 'X shaves X' are possible sentence-frames does not mean that there can be a barber who shaves all and only those who do not shave themselves.

In discussing Mackie's paradox Plantinga (1967, 168) considers a suggested definition of omnipotence different from those we have been criticizing:

X is omnipotent iff X is capable of performing any logically possible action.

This will not do, Plantinga says, because making a table that God did not make is a logically possible action, but God cannot make a table which God did not make. Nor can we say:

X is omnipotent iff X is capable of performing any action A such that the proposition 'X performs A' is logically possible.

For the unfortunate man who is capable only of scratching his ear is capable of performing any action A such that the proposition 'the man who is capable only of scratching his ear performs A' is logically possible, for the only such action A is the action of scratching his ear:

We might consider the suggestion that God is omnipotent iff God can do any A such that 'God does A' is logically possible.

This, of course, would not be a definition of omnipotence but only an explication of divine omnipotence. But even so, Plantinga remarks, it would be an unsuccessful explication. For let A be the action of 'doing what I am thinking of'. Then 'God does A' will be logically possible: it is logically possible for God to do what I am thinking of; but if what I am thinking of is creating a square circle, then God cannot do what I am thinking of.

Plantinga in the end abandons the search for a totally satisfactory account of omnipotence, believing rightly that such an account is not necessary in order to counter Mackie's argument. More recently Geach (1973, 7 ff.) has concluded, from difficulties such as the ones we have considered, that the notion of omnipotence is incapable of coherent formulation, and suggests that it be abandoned in favour of the notion of being *almighty*, i.e. as having power over all things. And Swinburne (1977, 156) thinks that in answer to puzzles like Mackie's we must say that an omnipotent being can indeed create a being which he cannot control, but that he can exercise this power only at the cost of thereby ceasing to be omnipotent.

I agree with Plantinga that it is difficult to formulate a coherent and elegant definition of omnipotence; and I agree with Geach that the notion of God as almighty is a more essential element in Western theism than the comparatively philosophical notion of omnipotence. But I think that an account of divine omnipotence simpler than Swinburne's can be devised to avoid the difficulties we have been discussing.

Let us consider the following definition of omnipotence: A being is omnipotent if it has every power which it is logically possible to possess.[1]

The definition must first of all be supplemented with an account of when it is logically possible to possess a power. It is logically possible to possess a power, I suggest, if the exercise of the power does not as such involve any logical impossibility. When I say that the exercise of the power does not *as such* involve any logical possibility I mean that there is no logical incoherence in the description of what it is to exercise the power. For a power to be a logically possible power it is not necessary that every exercise of it should be coherently conceivable, but only that some exercise of it should be.

I shall try to explain the definition, and bring out its merits, by applying it to some of the difficult cases current in the literature.

An omnipotent being can make an irresistible cannonball, and he can make an immovable lamp-post; there is nothing incoherent in the supposition that these powers are exercised. Of course there would be an incoherence in the idea of them both being exercised simultaneously; but our definition of the logical possibility

---

[1] The reader may be disappointed that this definition is not given quasi-logical form like the definitions rejected above. This is no accident. I have argued, in my paper 'Human Abilities and Logical Modalities' (Tuomela, 1974), that the current resources of logic are inadequate to analyse the relevant notion of power.

of possessing a power did not imply that every formulatable exercise of that power should be logically possible, but only that some should.

The man who is capable only of scratching his ear is not omnipotent by our definition; for there are many logically possible powers which he does not possess (e.g. the ability to create a world).

An omnipotent being has the power to do what I am thinking of. It is true that if I am thinking of something which it is impossible to do, then an omnipotent God cannot, on that occasion, exercise the power he has of doing what I am thinking about. But powers are not tied to particular occasions, and it is not necessary, for a power to be genuinely possessed, that it can be coherently exercised on all occasions and in all circumstances. Though God has the power to do what I am thinking of, he cannot exercise this power if I am thinking a nonsensical thought; just as, though he possesses the power to make an immovable lamp-post, he cannot exercise that power if he has just then exercised his power to make an irresistible cannonball.

It will be seen that the definition of omnipotence by generalizing over powers is an attempt to preserve the merits, without the disadvantages, of St. Thomas's formulation of omnipotence as infinite power. St. Thomas was, I think, right in saying that powers are manifested by their effects or, as he elsewhere puts it, specified by their exercises. That is to say, the power to ϕ can only be defined and understood by someone who knows what ϕ-ing is. But it is not true that powers are specified by their effects in such a way that an infinite power must have an infinite effect. No power, whether finite or infinite, is logically exhausted by its effect: even the human power to beget, with which Aquinas contrasts divine power, is not a limited power in the sense that the power to beget children is a power to beget some specified number of children.

There are advantages, then, in defining omnipotence as the totality of logically possible powers rather than as the power to perform all logically possible actions or to bring about all logically possible states of affairs. But even so defined as the totality of logically possible powers omnipotence cannot be ascribed to God. For there are many powers which it is logically possible to have which God cannot have, such as the power to make a table which God has not made. The power to change, to sin, and to die are instances of powers which it is logically possible to have—since we human beings have them—and yet which traditional theism denies to God.

Divine omnipotence, therefore, if it is to be a coherent notion, must be something less than the complete omnipotence which is the possession of all logically possible powers. It must be a narrower omnipotence, consisting in the possession of all logically possible powers which it is logically possible for a being with the attributes of God to possess. (If the definition is not to be empty 'attributes' must here be taken to mean those properties of Godhead which are not themselves powers: properties such as immutability and goodness.) This conception of divine omnipotence is close to traditional accounts of the doctrine while avoiding some of the incoherences we have found in them.

On this account, an omnipotent God will not have the power to make a table that God did not make. The power to make a table that one has not made is not a power that anyone can have; and the power to make a table that God did not make is not a power it is logically possible for someone to have who is identical with God. Any being with all the attributes of God will of course have, *inter alia*, the attribute of being identical with God.

What are we to say, on this account, in answer to the question whether an omnipotent God can make a being whom he cannot control? The power to create, while remaining omnipotent, a being that one cannot control is not a logically possible power, since the description of the power contains a hidden contradiction. The power to create a being that one cannot control and thereby give up one's omnipotence is not a power that could logically be possessed by a being who had the attributes of God including immutability. Consequently, the answer to the conundrum is in the negative: but this does not clash with the notion of divine omnipotence as we have now described it.

Powers such as the power to weaken, sicken, and die will not be parts of divine omnipotence since they clash with other divine attributes. What of the power to do evil? Clearly, the actual performance of an evil deed would be incompatible with divine goodness: but some theologians have thought that the mere power to do evil, voluntarily unexercised, is not only compatible with, but actually enhances the splendour of divine beneficence. If so, then the power to do evil, since it is clearly in itself a logically possible power, would be part of divine omnipotence. This is a topic to which we shall return. But in the immediately succeeding chapter, we must turn our attention to the question whether the power to bring about the past is a logically possible power, and therefore forms part of divine omnipotence.

VIII. OMNIPOTENCE AND TIME

In the fourth article of question twenty-five of the first part of the *Summa Theologiae* St. Thomas raises the question whether God can bring it about that the past should never have been. As is his custom, he presents three arguments for the answer which he is finally going to reject: in this case, three arguments for attributing to God the power to change the past. The first argument is that God can do things that are impossible in themselves, such as giving sight to the blind and life to the dead: *a fortiori* then he can do something whose impossibility arises merely from the incidental fact of its being dated at one time rather than another. The second argument is that God's power does not diminish, and so God must now be able to do whatever he was able to do in the past. But before Socrates ever ran, God could bring it about that he would not run: similarly, therefore, now that Socrates has run, God can bring it about that he has not run. The final argument depends on particular considerations about virginity. If a woman has lost her virginity, only a change in the past can make her a virgin again. But God can restore people to charity when they have lost it, and charity is more important than virginity, so *a fortiori* God can restore virginity.

Against these arguments St. Thomas first invokes the authority of St. Jerome, who wrote to the nun Eustochium, 'God who can do everything cannot restore a virgin after she has fallen.' This text had given rise to a famous discussion earlier in the Middle Ages in a dinner-table conversation between Desiderio of Cassino and St. Peter Damiani, recorded in the latter's *De Divina Omnipotentia*, which is printed in Migne's *Patrologia Latina* (vol. 145, 595 ff.). Peter Damiani maintained that Jerome was wrong; Desiderio said that he was right: God could not restore virgins, but only because he did not want to.

Damiani objected: 'If God cannot do any of the things that he does not want to do, since he never does anything except what he wants to do, it follows that he cannot do anything at all except what he does. As a result we shall have to say frankly that God is not making it rain today because he cannot.' This conclusion, he said, is surely absurd: we weak men can do many things that we do not do. There are indeed many things God cannot do, such as lying, but that is not because of any inability but because of his resolve of perpetual rectitude. Making a virgin out of a non-virgin, on the other hand, is not a bad thing to do, so there is no reason why God cannot do it.

The reason which Damiani himself gives for God's failing to restore virginity to those who have lost it suggests that what he had in mind was a physical operation rather than any genuine undoing of the past. God does not restore the marks of virginity to those who have lost them, he says, as a deterrent to lecherous young men and women, so that their sins will be more easily found out. But he goes on to consider an objection which is of greater interest from a logical point of view:

God can certainly destroy things that have been made, so that they exist no more: but it is impossible to see how he can bring it about that those things which were made should never have been made at all. He can bring it about that from now and henceforth Rome should no longer exist: but how can the opinion be maintained that he can bring it about that it should never have been built of old?

Aquinas, when he reaches this point in his consideration of the topic, argues that to bring about that the past should not have been is a contradictory feat: just as it involves a contradiction to say that Socrates is sitting and that he is not sitting, it involves a contradiction to say that he sat and that he did not sit. To say that he sat is to say that his sitting was in the past; to say that he did not sit is to say that it never was. It may be only incidental to Socrates' sitting or running that it was dated in the past; but it is not incidental to the past that what is past cannot be undone. It is not God's power that is diminished as time passes, but the number of possible things to do. God can restore a sinner to charity, but he cannot make him never have sinned any more than he can make a non-virgin never have lost her virginity.

Whether or not Aquinas's conclusion is correct, his argument seems to conflate together the distinction between a thing's being past and future and the distinction between a thing's actually happening and not actually happening. There are some things that did happen in the past, and some things that did not happen: the things that did not happen are in a sense just as past as those that did—that is to say, their not happening belongs to the past just as much as the happening of the things that did happen. Similarly, the future contains both what will happen and what will not happen: if something is *not* going to happen it is in the *future* that it is not going to happen. There is, of course, an enormous difference between things that happen and things that do not happen: only the former, for instance, can be genuinely individuated. But whether something is among the things that happen or among the things that do not happen is a separate matter from whether it belongs in the past, the present, or the future.

Damiani is quite clear about this. Having put to himself the difficulty, how can God bring it about that what is past should never have been, he replies:

As if this impossibility applied only to past things! There is a similar impossibility to be found in present and future times. For whatever is now the case, as long as it is the case, cannot not be the case. Likewise, what is future cannot not be future. But there are things which can come about or not come about with equal right: as that I should ride my horse today or not ride my horse; see my friend or not see my friend; that the weather should be clear or rainy. These are the kinds of things which those who are wise in the wisdom of this world call contingent.

Damiani is often accused in histories of philosophy and theology of saying that God could bring about self-contradictory states of affairs; but he is careful to point out that his view does not commit him to this:

Nothing can both be and not be; but what is not in the nature of things is undoubtedly nothing: you are a hard master, trying to make God bring about what is not his, namely nothing. It was he who gave this force of existence to things, so that once they have existed they cannot not have existed.

He did not believe, any more than Aquinas did, that God could undo what had been done; but to prove this he did not make the erroneous appeal that Aquinas made to the conditional necessity of what is the case. A careful reader of Damiani would realize that the correct way to introduce the discussion of God's power over the past is not to ask whether God can *change* the past, but whether he can *bring about* the past. Neither God nor anyone else can change the past, or change the future, if by this we mean change what has happened, or change what will happen. The real question is whether God can bring about the past in the way that we can bring about the future: whether, just as I can act now to bring about a future effect, God can act now to bring about a past effect.

Recently, Geach has argued against attributing to God power over the past. In his essay 'On praying for things to happen', he argues that one cannot rationally pray for something to *have* happened at the time of prayer (Geach, 1969, 89). This, he says, is not a matter of what God knows or can do, but a matter of what we can sensibly say. In using the imperative we represent a situation as still to be brought about, which is incompatible with representing it as a *fait accompli*.

But Geach's argument does not carry conviction. A defender of prayers for the past would say that if imperatives normally concern the future, that is because imperatives are normally addressed to human beings, and nothing need follow about imperatives addressed to God. After all, imperatives uttered to human beings have to be uttered aloud, but prayer may be said silently. Moreover, there is no reason why prayers should be said in the imperative only, rather than in the subjunctive or optative, which have a perfectly natural past tense: after all, the first three petitions of the Lord's Prayer are not in the imperative. Praying for the past is not an eccentricity of G. M. Hopkins and C. S. Lewis, as Geach implies: the Tridentine Mass included the prayer 'Deliver us, O Lord, from all evils past, present and to come.' If this prayer is nonsensical, or is to be given a meaning other than its obvious one, that is not because of considerations about the imperative mood, but because of limits on what God can sensibly be said to do.

It has been persuasively argued in our own time that there is nothing incoherent in the notion of causation acting backwards in time. Michael Dummett, in his paper 'Bringing about the Past' (1960), has shown that many of the arguments brought against the notion are fallacious. It is in the case of causal processes in which we intervene, Dummett says, unlike the motions of the starry heavens of which we are mere observers, that backwards causation seems particularly incredible:

When we consider ourselves as agents, and consider causal laws governing events in which we can intervene, the notion of backwards causality seems to generate absurdities. If an event C is considered the cause of a preceding event D, then it would be open to us to bring about C in order that the event D should have occurred. (Dummett, 1960, 316)

But even in such a case, Dummett argues, there is nothing genuinely incoherent in the notion.

Some theologians see something blasphemous in retrospective prayer—e.g. a prayer that my son should not have been drowned in a certain shipwreck of which I read in the newspapers. But why? This is not a prayer to the effect that if my son has been drowned God should now make him not to have drowned; I am asking that at the time of the disaster, he should then have made my son not to drown at that time. Such prayer may, of course, be rationalized not by appeal to a notion of backwards causation, but by an appeal to divine foreknowledge exercised in advance at the time of the shipwreck: 'God already knew then I was going to make this prayer and then granted it.'

There is a familiar argument against retrospective prayer: 'Either your son has drowned or not. If so, the prayer cannot be answered; if not it is superfluous.' This argument is as worthless as the fatalist argument against taking precautions: 'If you are fated to die, your precautions will be useless; if you are not, they will be wasted.' Any effective refutation of the fatalist will equally refute the argument to show that we cannot affect the past. On any sense of 'if' on which you can make the inference from 'you will not be killed' to 'If you do not take precautions, you will not be killed', it is impossible to pass from 'If you do not take precautions, you will not be killed' to 'Your taking precautions will not be effective in preventing your death.'

In order to bring out how it may be rational to act in order to bring about the past, without this involving any appeal to foreknowledge, Dummett invents a story. A certain tribe, each year, send their braves on a lion hunt in a distant region: they are absent for six days, during two of which they travel thither, two of which they hunt, and two of which they return home. While the braves are absent the chief dances in order to cause them to act bravely. He dances for all six days, not just for the first four; and he justifies this by saying that on the occasions in the past when chiefs have (either deliberately or by accident) danced for only four days the results have been disastrous.

How could we convince such a chief that his action was irrational? We may ask him: 'Why don't you dance after the young men have returned and you know they haven't acted bravely?' It seems we might argue as follows—either he does dance, in which case the dancing is proved not to be a sufficient condition of the previous bravery; or he does not (e.g. cannot move his limbs) so that the bravery must be a causal condition of the dancing. But this would be too simple a way to dispose of the claim about backwards causation. The chief may rationally reject a single counter-example or there may be a number of other, independent, explanations of his failure to dance.

Moreover, there is a third possible outcome, which is that it may later be discovered that on this occasion they were indeed brave and the reports of their cowardice had been false. If this happens often enough the chief will begin to trust his own intentions more than the reports of the returning braves. Dummett draws his moral:

My conclusion therefore is this. If anyone were to claim, of some type of action A (i) that experience gave grounds for holding the performance of A as increasing the probability of the previous occurrence of a type of event E and (ii) that experience gave grounds for regarding A as an action which it was ever not in his power to perform—that is, for entertaining the possibility of his trying to perform it and failing—then it would either force him to abandon one or other of those beliefs, or else to abandon the belief (iii) that it was ever possible for him to have knowledge, independent of his intention to perform A or not, of whether an event had occurred. Now doubtless most normal human beings would rather abandon (i) or (ii) than (iii) because we have the prejudice that (iii) must hold good for every type of case. But if someone were, in a particular case, more ready to give up (iii) than (i) or (ii) I cannot see any argument that one could use to dissuade him. (Dummett, 1960)

On Dummett's account, then, we have three competing propositions:

(1) A makes past E more probable
(2) A is in my power to perform
(3) I can know that E has occurred apart from my intention to perform A.

In the event of evidence which clashes with these three, we can choose which to withdraw; and hence we cannot say in advance that bringing about the past is impossible.

If bringing about the past is logically possible, then it seems that among the powers of an omnipotent being will be the power to bring about the past. Of course, God will not, even if he can bring about the past, make undone what is done; but then he cannot make unfuture the future either. The future is what will be the case when all alterations have been made, and neither God nor we can alter the future any more than we can alter the past.

Bringing about the future, like bringing about the past, is a different matter. But can God bring about the past? Was it not true in 754 BC that God could make it be that Rome was not founded, and now no longer true that he can prevent the foundation of Rome? If Dummett is right, we do not really know this. We know that God will not prevent the foundation of Rome since we know that Rome was founded; but it may be that he still can. In just the same way, I may know my own intention not to do X, and yet preserve the power to do X.

If Dummett is right, then there is nothing incoherent about prayer about the past, and its rationale need make no appeal to foreknowledge. Indeed, Dummett's theory, if correct, would itself make the problem of divine foreknowledge of future contingents more tractable. The principal difficulty in the matter was that if God foretold the sin of Judas in advance, then either Judas's sin must have been necessary in advance, or else God's foretelling concerned something in principle unforetellable. On Dummett's view, it may be that it is only after Judas has freely and contingently sinned that God causes the previous prediction of Judas's sin. God could thus be conceived as transcending time in the manner aimed at by the Boethian account of eternity, without the conception involving the incoherent consequences of that account.

Theological followers of Boethius have pictured God as surveying the battle-ground of human existence from a high tower above, with past, present, and future as different parts of the field open to the divine vision. If Dummett's account is correct, God should perhaps be pictured not as inhabiting a stationary tower, but as travelling from point to point of the field in a time machine.

Many philosophers with no particular theological bias have argued that the notion of a time machine is not an incoherent one. Some parapsychologists have believed—unlike Dummett—that not only God but human beings too have power to bring about the past, so that my present act of willing may make it be the case that the last card but two to be played was a knave.

Can an effect really precede its cause? If Hume's account of cause is the correct one, the notion of backward causation is a contradiction in terms; what distinguishes effect from cause is that of two events linked by constant conjunction the cause is the earlier and the effect the later. But there are grounds quite independent of any theological considerations for questioning the adequacy of Hume's account: there seems at least nothing incoherent in the notion of an effect that is simultaneous with its cause. But if we give up the demand that a cause should precede its effects in time, how are we to distinguish between cause and effect in a causal relation?

In Dummett's story the cause is a term in a causal relation which is under the direct control of a particular human agent (the mother's prayer, the chief's dance). Other recent philosophers have pointed out that it is possible to perform an act A in order to bring about an event E which is earlier in time than the performance of the act (e.g. Chisholm, 1960). In order to assist an experimenter to study patterns in my brain connected with certain muscular movements, for instance, I may raise my arm: the brain events are the cause, and not the effect, of the movement of the muscles involved in the arm-raising. But what examples such as these show is not that reverse causation is possible, but that the order of practical reasoning (the doing of A in order to bring about E) is not necessarily, as in the normal case, the same as the order of causation. If this is so, then the fact that one term of the causal relation is more immediately under the control of human beings will not show that to be the term which is the cause rather than the effect.

Dummett's account therefore leaves it unclear how we are to distinguish between cause and effect. More seriously, it seems to leave it enigmatic how we are to distinguish between earlier and later. Clearly, the distinction between earlier and later cannot here be drawn in terms of cause and effect; we cannot say that of two events if E1 is the cause and E2 the effect than E2 is later than E1. Nor indeed is it clear how we are to distinguish between past and future. For even if the world is not deterministic, we cannot, on Dummett's view, say that the future is distinguished from the past by being partially undetermined: for there are a number of past events of which there is not as yet a determining cause. And there is no reason for thinking of the past as already 'there' in any way in which the future is not: if there can be propositions with truth-values whose truth-values we cannot determine, there is no reason why these should be exclusively past-tensed rather than future-tensed propositions.

It may be said that the question 'How are we to distinguish between past and future?' is an absurd one: it is not as if we could ever be in a situation in which we could identify a certain event for the event it is, and then have to go on to inquire: 'Now is this a past event, or a future event?' This, I think, is correct: but the difficulty with Dummett's account is precisely that it does make it look as if such a situation were genuinely possible.

We sometimes picture the course of time and history as a book which is open at a single page, the present. This picture is used in different ways by determinists and indeterminists. On one view, the future is a book already written, but the book is open only at the present page, and we do not see what is yet to come until we turn the leaf. On the other view, the future pages are not yet written—at the very least they contain substantial blanks—and it is only as we turn the leaves that by our free action we write into the blanks and fill the pages of the book.

Now on Dummett's view, there are not only pages later in the book but also pages earlier in the book that contain blanks: we can not only turn forward the pages and fill in the blanks, but turn back a page or two and fill in a blank there too. This picture, and the theory behind it, seems coherent only if we imagine this turning back as something exceptional: if there were a large number of causal relationships running backwards in the world, it would become difficult to operate with the scheme of past, present, and future at all. In the simile of the open book, after a while there ceases to be a clear sense in which we can talk about 'the page of the book that now lies open'; when the sense of that is lost then so is the sense of past, present, and future. In Dummett's story there was not universal two-way causation; there was a single cause working backwards, and it was assumed that other causal relations operated in the normal manner. The plausibility of the story depended crucially on that assumption.

The difficulty is less palpable if we imagine backwards causation as a divine prerogative, so that finite causes all work in one direction and there is just one single, infinite, eternal cause capable of effecting the past. But if we imagine God as exercising reverse causation as frequently as would be necessary to provide an explanation of omniscient foreknowledge of free human actions then the distinction between past and future again becomes blurred. Dummett's account in the end seems to founder on the same difficulty as Boethius's. In a world governed by the universal operation of divine reverse causality, no less than in a world in which every event is simultaneous with the whole of a divine eternity, the notion of two events being at the same time as each other seems to lose any sharp sense.

IX. OMNIPOTENCE AND GOODNESS

Theologians commonly agree that omnipotence does not include the power to do wrong. To sin is to fail to act perfectly, said Aquinas; so the power to sin is the power to fail in action, which is the opposite of omnipotence; so that though God is omnipotent he cannot sin. You can say, if you like, 'God can do wicked things if he wishes': this is a conditional whose truth depends on the impossibility of its antecedent and its consequent, like 'If a man is a donkey he has four legs.' To prove to the Arminians that virtuous action could be praiseworthy though necessitated, Jonathan Edwards appealed to their own admission that God was necessarily holy and his will necessarily determined to that which is good. Only a few eccentrics have argued that it must be strictly speaking possible for God to do something wicked, since otherwise he would not be a free agent and his goodness would not be matter for praise.

But among those who have agreed that God is not free to do wrong, there has been disagreement how far he enjoys freedom at all to act otherwise than he has done. One of the earliest, and still one of the most interesting, contributions to the debate was that of Abelard. In the fifth chapter of his *Introduction to Theology* Book III (printed in Migne's *Patrologia Latina*, vol. 178, pp. 1094–1103) Abelard discusses the question whether God can make more things, or better things, than the things he has made and whether he can refrain from acting as he does. The question, he says, seems difficult to answer either with a yes or with a no.

On the one hand, if God can make more and better things than those he has made, is he not mean not to do so: after all it costs him no effort! Whatever he does or refrains from doing is done or left undone for the best possible reasons, however hidden from us these may be. Whatever he has done has been right and just: hence it would be unjust for him to have left it undone. So it seems that God cannot act except in the way he has in fact acted.

On the other hand, if we take any sinner on his way to damnation, it is clear that he could be better than he is: for if not, he is not to be blamed, still less damned, for his sins. We know, that is, that it is true to say of him:

> This sinner can be saved by God.

We know also that:

> This sinner will be saved by God if and only if God saves this sinner.

So surely we can conclude:

> God can save this sinner,

even in a case where *de facto* the sinner is going to be damned. So there are at least some things which God can do apart from those which at some time or other he in fact does.

Abelard himself opts for the first horn of this dilemma. Suppose, he says, that it is not now raining. Then it is because God so wills that it is not now raining. That must mean that it is not now a suitable time for rain. So if we say that God could now make it rain, we are attributing to God the power to do something foolish. Whenever God wants to do something, he can do it; but when he does not wish to do something (because it would be wrong to do so) then he lacks also the power to do it.

Abelard knows that this opinion is an unpopular one among theologians. They say that it is offensive to the grandeur of God: even we poor creatures can act otherwise than we do. But Abelard replies that the power to act otherwise is not something to be proud of: it is a mark of our infirmity, like our ability to walk, eat, and commit sin. We would be much better off if we could only do what we ought to do. Some theologians say that God can act otherwise than he does in the sense that if he did, nothing would prevent him. But in that sense, Abelard retorts, we might as well say that God can commit sin.

To counter the argument that sinners must be capable of salvation if they are to be justly punished, Abelard mounts an attack on the underlying modal principle according to which '*p* iff *q*' entails " 'possibly *p*' entails 'possibly *q*' ". He produces a series of counter-examples against the principle: a sound may be audible, for instance, without there being anyone to hear it; hence, Abelard says, the following proposition is true:

This sound is heard by someone iff someone hears this sound while the following proposition is false:

It is possible for this sound to be heard by someone iff it is possible for someone to hear this sound.

(If, for instance, the sound is loud enough to be audible, but there is no-one not deaf in earshot.)

Abelard is prepared for the objection that God would deserve no gratitude from men if he cannot do other than he does. It is not, he says, as if God is acting under compulsion: his will is identical with the nature and goodness which necessitates him to act as he does. Like many later compatibilists in a different context, he insists that liberty of spontaneity is enough to make God's actions voluntary without there being any need for liberty of indifference.

Finally Abelard clears away the objection that if God can only do things at that optimum time at which he does them, his omnipotence must vary from time to time and his nature is no longer unchangeable. We must distinguish between attaching temporal qualifications to the exercise of a power, and attaching them to the power itself. If t is the only suitable time for doing X, then we can say truly of God:

God can do-X-only-at-t.

But it would be false to say:

Only-at-t-can God do X.

The temporal qualifications which can be attached to the exercise of divine power, Abelard says, are parallel to the spatial qualifications attached to exercises of human power. Of a human being we can say:

He cannot swim-when-he-is-on-dry-land

without being obliged to conclude:

When-he-is-on-dry-land he cannot swim.

Abelard's discussion is an astonishing exhibition of dialectical brilliance, introducing or reinventing a number of distinctions which are of great importance in modal logic and the logic of ability: but it cannot be said to amount to a credible account of omnipotence. The distinctions drawn between powers and their exercise apply only in the case of beings of limited capacity where there is room for a distinction between ability and opportunity; the ability to do whatever one desires is not sufficient for omnipotence but is achievable by finite beings with sufficient self-control to limit their wants to fit their scope. Because liberty of indifference is necessary for voluntariness, or rather because wants cannot be attributed to beings which do not have the ability to act in more than one way, Abelard's God lacks not only omnipotence but also the power of voluntary action: lacking that, he cannot be a person at all.

Abelard's theory of omnipotence was bitterly attacked by St. Bernard, and in 1140 the Council of Sens condemned the proposition that God can act and refrain from acting only in the manner and at the time that he actually does act and refrain from acting, and in no other way.[1] Henceforth Catholic theologians accepted that God could act otherwise than he does in fact act.

Aquinas explained how this was to be reconciled with the truth that God can do only what is fitting and just to do:

The words 'fitting and just' can be understood in two senses. In the first sense 'fitting and just' is taken in primary conjunction with the verb 'is', and thus restricted in reference to the present world, and is assigned to God's power in this restricted sense. With this restriction the proposition is false: for its sense is this: God can do only what is fitting and just as things are. But if 'fitting and just' is taken in primary conjunction with the verb 'can', which has an amplificatory force, and only subsequently in conjunction with the verb 'is', then the reference will be to a non-specific present, and the proposition will be true, understood in the sense: God can do only what, if He did it, would be fitting and just. (*S.Th.* Ia, 25, 5, 2)[2]

---

[1] 'Quod ea solummodo possit Deus facere vel dimittere, vel eo modo tantum, vel eo tempore, quo facit et non alio' (Denzinger, 1952, 374).

[2] Cum dicitur quod Deus non potest facere nisi quod ei est conveniens et iustum, potest intelligi dupliciter. Uno modo, sic quod hoc quod dico *conveniens et iustum,* prius intelligatur coniungi cum hoc verbo *est,* ita quod restringatur ad standum pro praesentibus; et sic referatur ad potentiam. Et sic falsum est quod dicitur: est enim sensus: *Deus non potest facere nisi quod modo conveniens est et iustum.* Si vero prius coniungatur cum hoc verbo *potest,* quod habet vim ampliandi, et postmodum cum hoc verbo *est,* significabitur quoddam praesens confusum: et erit locutio vera, sub hoc sensu: *Deus non potest facere nisi id quod, si faceret, esset conveniens et iustum.'*

This acute but obscure passage is perhaps best clarified in the contemporary idiom of possible worlds. Suppose we call the possible world which, as things are, is actual by the name 'alpha'. If a different possible world were actual, then, in this idiom, 'alpha' would no longer be the name of the actual world. The distinction that Aquinas is making can then be put as follows. Whichever possible world is actual, the following proposition would be true:

Whatever God has done is fitting and just in the actual world.

But the following proposition would not necessarily be true:

Whatever God has done is fitting and just in alpha.

Indeed, in worlds very different from alpha, it would very likely be false.

Aquinas puts to himself the question whether God has the power to make better what he has made. His answer is subtle and nuanced. If 'better' is taken as an adverb, the answer is definitely 'no': God has made everything he has made in the wisest and best possible way. If we take 'better' as an adjective, then we have to distinguish: we have to distinguish between essential and accidental properties of the things that God has made. Suppose, for instance, that we ask whether God could have made men better. If we mean 'could God have made human nature better than it is' the answer must be in the negative: creatures that were by nature better than we are by nature might be more estimable creatures, but they would not be human beings at all. On the other hand, it is true of any individual human being that God could have made him a better man than he is; and it is also true that given any specific creature of God, God could have made a better creature than that —even the most exalted angelic nature did not exhaust his power of creating excellence.

Aquinas, therefore, was far from believing that this was the best of all possible worlds. He did not even believe that this world was in the best of all its possible states. No doubt each kind of creature in the world was made as well as it could possibly have been made, so that if a world is individuated by the kind of creatures that exist in it, the actual world could not have been a better world. But each individual creature in the world could have been a better creature of that kind than it is, and each kind of creature could have been bettered, in another creatable world, by another and superior kind of creature.

Leibniz, as is well known, believed that this was the best of all possible worlds. In the eighth chapter of the first part of his *Theodicy* he says that God's supreme wisdom, conjoined with a no less infinite goodness, could not have failed to choose the best. A lesser good is a kind of evil, just as a lesser evil is a kind of good; so God must have chosen the best world under pain of having done evil. If there were no best world, he would not have chosen to create at all. It may appear that a world without sin and suffering would have been better, but that is an illusion: if the slightest of its existing evils were lacking in the present world, it would be a different world; since the eternal truths demand that physical and moral evil are possible, there are many of the infinitely many possible worlds which contain them, and it may well be that the best of all worlds is among those which do so. God is infinitely powerful, but power joined to wisdom can produce only the best: this does not constrain God or necessitate his choice. God can do anything which does not entail a contradiction: but to make something which will be better than the best itself is to achieve a contradictory feat.

Leibniz distinguishes his own position from that of Abelard whom he affects to consider as a quibbler on the topic of omnipotence. Unlike Abelard he claims that other worlds besides the actual world are possible—metaphysically possible, that is; the necessity which obliged God to chose the best world was not metaphysical but moral necessity. Abelard in his turn, it seems, could have replied that to speak of a possibility which not even an omnipotent God could actualize was indeed to quibble.

The dispute between those who, like Abelard and Leibniz, think that God must have chosen the best world, and those who, like Aquinas, think that God must have chosen a good world but could have chosen other better ones, is a reflection within natural theology of a dispute which is familiar to contemporary philosophers in the field of ethics. We are used to a controversy between partisans of the right and partisans of the good. For utilitarians, and for many other modern thinkers, there is at each juncture a single action which is right and morally obligatory: for instance, the action with the most felicific consequences. This conception is alien to most traditional Christianity which had a law-like notion of morality. According to this doctrine, at any given time there would be for each agent a number of actions forbidden and morally excluded; but save in exceptional circumstances there was not just one permissible action or one obligatory action. Similarly, in matters where the criminal law operates, there are usually many options open to us which are illegal, and many which are legal; in most circumstances there is not one single action which is obliged on us by law.

The morality by which Abelard and Leibniz judge the divinity is a morality of rightness, not of goodness. This is stated explicitly enough by Abelard, who does not seem to have been conscious of the number of questions begged in its formulation. Clearly, if one believes that God is not free to do anything wrong, and that at any given point there is only one action which is right for a moral agent, then one must conclude that God is not free to take any course of action other than one.

It was common ground to Abelard, Aquinas, and Leibniz that God could do no wrong: each of them, therefore, had a problem in accounting for the moral and physical evil in the universe. The problem of evil might seem more intractable for those who accept a morality of rightness: they have to prove, in the face of the visible evil around us, that God made not only a good world, but the best of all possible worlds. But acceptance of an ethic of rightness often goes with some form of consequentialism, with an acceptance of the principle that the end justifies the means. Leibniz, for instance, while insisting that fallible creatures like ourselves have to obey rules come what may, since we are more certain of the badness of certain means than we are of their success in producing good ends, exempts God from an absolute requirement of the same kind. A consequentialist ethic finds it easier than a legalistic ethic to justify evil in the cause of good. A legalistic ethic on the other hand cannot justify means by ends: if any action of God was bad by absolute standards, it could not be justified by saying that it formed part of a good universe, any more than a murder committed by a human being could be justified by a good end.

The Leibnizian approach is well expressed in a famous section of Pope's *Essay on Man*:

Of Systems possible, if 'tis confest
That Wisdom infinite must form the best. . . .
Respecting Man, whatever wrong we call,
May, must be right, as relative to all. . . .
All Nature is but Art, unknown to thee:
All Chance, Direction, which thou canst not see;
All Discord, Harmony, not understood;
All partial Evil, universal Good:
And, spite of Pride, in erring Reason's spite,
One truth is clear, 'Whatever is, is RIGHT.'

There lines are often taken as typical of Christian theodicy; in fact their substance would have been firmly rejected by theologians such as Aquinas. Whether Aquinas or Leibniz had the correct approach to the relationship between omnipotence and goodness is not something to be settled by natural theology alone. As we saw in the second chapter that different views on the divine knowledge of eternal truths were reflections of different theories of the nature of logical truth, so here we see that different accounts of the divine power to do good reflect different conceptions of the nature of moral goodness. As in the second chapter where we were happy to leave the resolution of the dispute to the philosophers of mathematics, so here we may leave the theological problem to wait on the progress of moral philosophy. Neither there nor here does the introduction of the theological aspect make the philosophical problem harder or easier to resolve.

CONCLUSION

X. THE GOD OF REASON AND THE GOD OF FAITH

If the argument of the previous chapters has been correct then there is no such being as the God of traditional natural theology: the concept of God propounded by scholastic theologians and rationalist philosophers is an incoherent one. If God is to be omniscient, I have argued, then he cannot be immutable. If God is to have infallible knowledge of future human actions, then determinism must be true. If God is to escape responsibility for human wickedness, then determinism must be false. Hence in the notion of a God who foresees all sins but is the author of none, there lurks a contradiction. Omnipotence may perhaps be capable in isolation, of receiving a coherent formulation; but omnipotence, while capable of accounting for some historic doctrines of pre-destination, is inadequate as a foundation for divine foreknowledge of undetermined human conduct. There cannot, if our argument has been sound, be a timeless, immutable, omniscient, omnipotent, all-good being.

The inquiry we have undertaken has been a very limited one. Only two of the traditional divine attributes were singled out for detailed treatment. If these are incompatible with other properties ascribed to God, that is, of course, enough to show that nothing can possess the totality of the divine attributes. But other attributes—such as that of being creator of heaven and earth—may justly be regarded as being more essential than omnipotence and omniscience to the traditional religious notion of God; and these we have not considered.

John Stuart Mill, reflecting on the problem set by the presence of evil and good in the world, came to the conclusion that it could only be solved by acknowledging the existence of God but denying divine omnipotence. He concluded his essay *Theism* in the following manner:

These, then, are the net results of natural theology on the question of the divine attributes. A being of great but limited power, how or by what limited we cannot even conjecture; of great and perhaps unlimited intelligence, but perhaps also more narrowly limited power than this, who desires, and pays some regard to, the happiness of his creatures, but who seems to have other motives of action which he cares more for, and who can hardly be supposed to have created the universe for that purpose alone. Such is the deity whom natural religion points to, and any idea of God more captivating than this comes only from human wishes, or from the teaching of either real or imaginary revelation . . . (Mill, 1887, 194)

It may well be argued that the deity of Mill's natural religion differs no more than the deity of scholastic and rationalist philosophy does from the God of Abraham, Isaac, and Jacob described in the Scriptures. Certainly none of the arguments developed in the present work would rule out the existence of a God with the attributes described in the quoted passage.

No account has been taken in the present work of arguments for the existence of God. If it is correct that the God of traditional natural theology is inconceivable, then there must be a flaw in arguments to establish his existence. None of the arguments in fact offered for the existence of God appear to me to be sound: nor, on the other hand, do the arguments of Hume and Kant to show that there cannot be a proof even of a God conceived in the manner of Mill.

Whether such a divine being is conceivable is not easy to decide. When we ask whether God is conceivable, we have to bear in mind the question: what is the test of something's being conceivable? A notion is conceivable only if it is free from contradiction: that much is sure; but Kant, Wittgenstein, and the positivists have suggested other, more stringent, criteria of conceivability. The conditions laid down by those philosophers seem to be unsatisfactory for reasons unconnected with theism; but they are right to say that freedom from contradiction is only a necessary and not a sufficient condition for conceivability. Certainly it must be insufficient if any argument from the condition of the world to the existence of God is to be valid: for few proponents of the cosmological argument would claim that it was actually self-contradictory to maintain that the world came into existence out of nothing.

If any being is to be identified with the God of traditional religious theism then clearly, even if he is not omniscient and omnipotent, his knowledge and power must be immeasurably superior to those of human beings; and his knowledge and power must not be limited by the laws of nature which operate in the material world. Is it possible to conceive of a being which has no body but which has a mind whose sphere of operation is the whole universe?

The minds we know are embodied minds. The mental predicates we learn to predicate are attached to subjects who are, or have, bodies. We attribute thoughts to them on the basis of what they say with their lips and make with their hands and do with their bodies. It is not, of course, only to human bodies that we can attribute mental predicates. We attribute thoughts of a simple kind to animals. When my dog sees me go to the can-opener at the appropriate time of day he behaves in such a way that it is perfectly natural to say that he thinks that I am going to feed him. Some people are as happy to attribute thoughts of a complicated kind to computers as I am to attribute thoughts of a simple kind to my dog. The attribution of thoughts to the computers we know commonly betrays confusion about the nature of thought; but I do not wish to deny that thoughts can be attributed to things made of very different kinds of hardware. There is no reason why one has to be made of flesh and blood to have thoughts, and I see no reason to deny *a priori* that an artefact might have thoughts. Indeed, how do I know that I was not myself made in a laboratory? Not by any argument 'I think, therefore I am not an artefact.'

If we are inclined to attribute thoughts and knowledge to computers it is because they can acquire, store, and communicate information. But the storage of information is not the same as the possession of knowledge; if it were, railway schedules would know the times of trains. It is because computers do not exhibit the information they contain in behaviour in pursuit of self-selected goals of the appropriate kind that their information-storing capacities do not count as knowledge. Computers are not alive, and only living beings can think.

We attribute knowledge to animals on the basis of our observation of their behaviour coupled with our knowledge of their repertoire, of their needs, and their sensory capacities. The attribution of knowledge to a being goes hand in hand with the attribution of desire and power to it; but of course the kind of knowledge, desire, and power differs from case to case—to animals we attribute perception, appetite, and various abilities, but not intuition, will, and choice.

Our attribution of these to humans is itself based on behaviour and paradigmatically on linguistic behaviour. The propositions that I think, qua propositions, do not belong to any one person rather than another; many a man can have the thought that 2 and 2 make 4 or that the sun is greater than the moon. What makes my thoughts *my* thoughts is such things as that they are expressed by my mouth and written by my hand. If there is a God, who has thoughts, what makes the thoughts *his* thoughts? If God has no body, then there is no divine bodily behaviour to serve as the basis of attribution to him of thoughts and knowledge.

In some philosophical traditions the immateriality of God makes it easier, not harder, to believe that he has thoughts. For Plato and the Platonists there is a special affinity between an immaterial God and the immaterial Ideas that are the real object of whatever knowledge anyone has. Aristotle and the Aristotelians too have made a close link between knowledge and immateriality: indeed, Aquinas accepted the theorem that immateriality entails knowledge. Thus, in answering the question whether God has knowledge, Aquinas writes:

The immateriality of any being is the reason why it has cognition; and the type of its cognition corresponds to the type of immateriality. In *De Anima II* it is said that plants have no cognition because of their materiality. A sense is a cognitive power because it receives ideas without matter; and the understanding is even more cognitive because it is more separate from matter and unmixed, as it is said in *De Anima* III. Thus, since God is at the highest point of immateriality, it follows that he is at the highest point of cognition. (*S.Th.* Ia, 14, 1)

Most contemporary philosophers find immateriality a much more problematic concept, and find it hard to conceive an immaterial knower. Can a disembodied have thoughts, or, what comes to the same thing, is a disembodied mind possible?

Peter Geach has raised this question, and illuminated it with an instructive example:

Let us imagine that over a period of time a roulette wheel gives only the numbers 1 to 26, and that this sequence of numbers spells out English sentences according to the obvious code (A=1, B=2, etc.) Let us further imagine that this goes on although the most elaborate precautions are taken against physical tampering with the wheel. All of this is clearly possible and raises no conceptual difficulties. I submit that we could then have conclusive evidence that the thoughts normally expressible by the English sentences in question were being originated,

and strong evidence that they were originated by no living organism. . . .
This and the like examples can show the possibility of disembodied
thought; thought unconnected with any living organism. (1969, 39)

There are difficulties about this example, and Geach recognizes
that in the case envisaged there seems no clear way of answering
the question *how many* minds are at work; the example suggests
no criterion for the identification and individuation of disembodied
minds. But why, faced with such a situation, should one say that
we have here a disembodied mind at all? No doubt we would be
right to reject the idea that here we have a roulette wheel which,
unlike other roulette wheels, has the power to think. But why
should we not say that this roulette wheel is being worked upon by
another embodied mind through some unknown force? It seems
that there can be no reason for rejecting in advance non-material
modes of agency which is not at least as good a reason for rejecting
non-material substances or minds.

In the case of God, a theist might say, we need not try to answer
the question *how many* divine persons there are. Aquinas and other
theologians have thought that all that the light of reason could
show was that the divine nature was instantiated. The question
'How many persons share the divine nature?' was a different one;
the correct answer (namely three) could be given only by revelation.
And of course Geach's example was not at all meant to show how
one would go about to prove that there are disembodied minds,
but only to give content to the notion that thoughts might be
expressed with no organism expressing them.

The work of a disembodied mind might perhaps also be
exhibited in the ingenious construction of an artefact not itself
carried out by human hand or artefact. If, say, my typewriter
divided itself into small pieces of metal, and then formed itself
into a clock before my eyes, I might well be inclined to say that
a disembodied mind was at work, though again I might cast about
for alternative descriptions of what had happened.

The two types of illustration of the notion of a disembodied
mind are analogous to the traditional notions of the revealed and
natural word of God. The revealed word of God was conceived as
a linguistic expression of the infinite knowledge of God: whether
produced miraculously (as in the writing on the wall at Belshazzar's
feast) or by normal human efforts of composition (like the Epistles
of St. Paul). The natural word of God was the world itself, con-

sidered as God's creation and as an expression of God's intelligence.

The world was not thought of as the expression of God's mind in the way that our words and actions are the expression of our thoughts. To think in that way would be to make the world God's body, which traditional theology would have regarded as objectionably pantheistic. Such pantheism has found an echo in recent philosophy. Arthur Danto, in an influential article (Danto, 1965), has introduced the notion of a *basic action*. A basic action is an action which one does not by doing anything else; I may wind my watch by moving my finger and thumb, but it is not by doing something else that I move my finger and thumb. Danto suggests that a body can be defined as the locus of one's basic actions. If God can act in the world directly and without intermediary, as traditionally he has been held to, then on Danto's definition the world would be God's body. Most traditional theologians would have rejected this idea with horror.

The universe has traditionally been regarded as an expression of God's knowledge not in the way that our bodily movements express our knowledge but in the way that a work of art is an expression of an artist's skill. Most artists work with their hands: if the world is an artefact of God's mind, there is nothing which comes between the craftsman's mind and his work as a human craftsman's hands do. But is it a contingent or a necessary matter that the craftsmen and artists we know work with their hands? If a poet were gifted with telekinetic powers, could he not think his poems direct on to Geach's roulette wheel?

Some people have claimed to have the ability to work metal and sculpt figures merely by taking thought; and some philosophers have believed them. Let us assume that such claims are true: even so, they do not provide a parallel for the relation between a creator and the world. For even in telekinesis the agent is identified by being a particular body in a particular place: the agent who makes the claims to have unusual powers, and whose predictions are, if he is fortunate, fulfilled, is a normal bodily agent. If we thought that even the lips of the wonder-worker were being operated by telekinesis then all reason to attribute the remote effects to *his* agency would disappear. But in the case of a non-embodied agent whose sphere of immaterial operation is the entire universe there seems no parallel Archimedean point from which the concept of agency can get a purchase.

I know of no successful treatment of the philosophical problems involved in conceiving a non-embodied mind active throughout the universe: it is indeed rare to find among theistic philosophers even an attempt to solve the problems. I would certainly not claim to know that the problems are insoluble; in the present chapter I have only hinted at their nature: to set them out in full would take a different book. But in the presence of the difficulties, and in the absence of even the offer of a plausible solution to them, it would seem to me to be a rash person who would claim to know that there is a God.

I suppose that few people claim to know that there is a God; most believe it as a matter of faith. But traditionally faith was faith in God as saviour, not as creator; it was faith, not in the existence of God, but in the promises of a God whose existence was taken as so obvious that only ill will could account for the failure to recognize it. Faith was demanded in God's promises to his chosen people, or in his revelation to Jesus, not in there being a God who could promise or reveal. Even against such a background it is no easy matter to show that such faith is reasonable; without such a background its rationality is even more difficult to establish. The absolute commitment demanded by religious traditions is a deliberate giving of assent beyond what the evidence demands. The justification of this is the most important task for the theist philosopher of religion.

Someone might ask a question in the spirit of Kierkegaard: 'Suppose that the philosophical difficulties about the attributes of God were all cleared up: suppose that the Five Ways, or the onto-logical argument, were shown to be valid—would it then be any more reasonable than now to give the absolute commitment? Take any philosophical argument you conceive to be valid—say, the argument against private languages, or the refutation of the naturalistic fallacy or whatever is your favourite—would it be reasonable to commit one's whole way of life to its validity?' If the answer to these questions is no, as it surely must be, then surely philosophical questions about the nature and existence of God must be irrelevant to faith.

The Kierkegaardian point shows only the insufficiency of the philosophical justification of an option for or against belief in God; it does not impugn its necessity. Its purpose, of course, was to act as an imaginative test of the sincerity of philosophical doubts.

But if the validity or invalidity of arguments for and against the existence of God is wholly irrelevant to faith, then faith seems a vicious habit of mind, a turning of one's back on the possibility of discovering truth.

But granted that the philosophical questions are relevant, can any man seriously hope to see them definitely settled in his lifetime? Given the philosophical uncertainty how should we behave? Some men believe themselves to have a direct experience of God, which would shut out the need for a proof of his existence. Most men claim no such experience, and indeed given the nature traditionally ascribed to God it is arguable that no such experience is possible. Others claim to see in a Scripture, or a religious community, marks so clear of divine revelation as to provide by themselves a justification for belief in God.

This position becomes less reasonable each time that church leaders hasten to abandon those parts of their message which make it distinguishable from the current fashion in secular reasoning, or whenever religious traditions come to regard the Scriptures as being no more inspired than the works of Plato. But of course the religious retreat before secular pressures and the religious adoption of secular values may well itself be a temporary fashion. Certainly it would be wrong to argue that one could never be justified in accepting something as a message from X unless one had independent reasons for believing in the existence of X; a message from Mars might make one believe in the existence of living beings on Mars which there was no other reason to suspect.

It may indeed be that the existence of God is, as St. Paul thought it was, something so obvious that only ill will or philosophical perversity could prevent one from seeing it. That something is denied by very many people is no proof that it is not obvious; and there is no lack of parallel examples of philosophically induced blindness. For centuries philosophers doubted the existence of the external world and lamented the lack of proof of the existence of other minds. To many of us, the arguments that led them to doubt these obvious truths now seem archaic sophistries. As for ill will, there is no lack of evidence of that. Anyone who has once believed in God and does so now no longer has no difficulty in pointing to events in his own life and vices in his own character which may have darkened his vision and perverted his judgement. We have all reason to fear the judgements of

God and therefore to wish away the existence of a divine judge.

Ill will, however, can corrupt the judgement in more ways than one: the belief of a believer may be the effect of his vices as the unbelief of an unbeliever may be. And scepticism about the external world is self-destructive in a way quite different from scepticism about the existence of God. For practical atheism is a possibility whereas practical solipsism is not.

One thing seems clear. There is no reason why someone who is in doubt about the existence of God should not pray for help and guidance on this topic as in other matters. Some find something comic in the idea of an agnostic praying to a God whose existence he doubts. It is surely no more unreasonable than the act of a man adrift in the ocean, trapped in a cave, or stranded on a mountainside, who cries for help though he may never be heard or fires a signal which may never be seen.

Such prayer seems rational whether or not there is a God; whether, if there is a God, it is pleasing to him or conducive to salvation is quite another question. Religious people, no doubt, will have their own views about that. But if there is a God, then surely prayer for enlightenment about his existence and nature cannot be less pleasing to him than the attitude of a man who takes no interest in a question so important, or in a question so difficult would not welcome assistance beyond human powers.

BIBLIOGRAPHY

Unless otherwise indicated below, works are cited in the text by name of author, year of publication, and page.

Ackrill, J. L., 1963, *Aristotle's 'Categories' and 'De Interpretatione'*, Oxford.

Adams, R. M., 1977, 'Middle Knowledge and the Problem of Evil', *American Philosophical Quarterly*, 14.

Anscombe, G. E. M., 1963, *Intention*, Oxford.

——, 1956, 'The Sea Battle' *Mind*, 65.

——, 1975, 'The First Person', in Guttenplan, *Mind and Language*, London.

Aquinas, St. Thomas, *Summa contra Gentiles*, Turin–Rome, 1934.

——, *Summa Theologiae*, Latin and English text, Blackfriars edn. London, 1963–; cited as '*S.Th.*' followed by number of part, question, and article.

——, *Quaestiones Disputatae de Potentia Dei*, Turin–Rome, 1949.

Baudry, L., 1950, *La Querelle des Futurs Contingents (Louvain, 1465–75)*, Paris.

Berkeley, George, 1954, *Three Dialogues*, ed. C. Turbayne, Indianapolis.

Castañeda, H. N., 1967, 'Omniscience and Indexical Reference', *Journal of Philosophy*, 64.

Celluprica, V., 1977, *Il capitolo 9 del 'de Interpretatione' di Aristotele*, Rome.

Chisholm, R., 1960, 'Making Things to have Happened', *Analysis*.

Chomsky, N., 1968, *Language and Mind*, New York.

Copleston, F., 1953, *A History of Philosophy, Ockham to Suarez*, London.

Damiani, St. Peter, 1943, *De Divina Omnipotentia ed altri opuscoli*, ed. F. Brizzi, Rome.

Danto, A., 1965, 'Basic Actions', *Philosophical Quarterly*.

Denzinger H., 1952, *Enchiridion Symbolorum*, Freiburg.

Descartes, R., *Œuvres*, ed. C. Adam and P. Tannery, Paris, 1964–; cited as 'AT' followed by volume and page number.

——, *Philosophical Works*, trans. E. Haldane and G. T. Ross; Cambridge, 1967; cited as 'HR' followed by volume and page number.

——, *Philosophical Letters*, trans. A. Kenny, Oxford, 1970; cited as 'K' followed by page number.

Dummett, M., 1959, 'Wittgenstein's Philosophy of Mathematics', *Philosophical Review*.

——, 1960, 'On Bringing about the Past', *Philosophical Review*.

Edwards, J., 1959, *The Freedom of the Will*, ed. P. Ramsey, Princeton.

Flew, A. G. N., 1966, *God and Philosophy*, London.

——, and McIntyre, A. C., 1955, *New Essays in Philosophical Theology*, London.

Geach, P. T., 1969, *God and the Soul*, London.

——, 1966, *Descartes' Philosophical Writings*, London (with G. E. M. Anscombe).

——, 1973, 'Omnipotence', *Philosophy*.

——, 1977, *Providence and Evil*, Cambridge.

Gibieuf, P., 1630, *De Libertate Dei et Creaturae*, Paris.

Hunt, R. W., 1943, 'Studies on Priscian', *Medieval and Renaissance Studies*.

Kenny, A., 1969a, *Aquinas, a Collection of Critical Essays*, London.

——, 1969b, *The Five Ways*, London.

——, 1976, *Will, Freedom and Power*, Oxford.

——, 1978, *Freewill and Responsibility*, London.

Kretzmann, N., 1966, 'Omniscience and Immutability', *Journal of Philosophy*, 63.

Lemmon, E. J., 1966, 'Sentences, Statements and Propositions', in *British Analytical Philosophy*, ed. B. A. O. Williams and A. Montefiore, London.

Lucas, J., 1970, *The Freedom of the Will*, Oxford.

Luther, M., *'De Servo Arbitrio'*. References are to the standard edition, the *Weimarer Ausgabe*, cited 'WA'; translations are by Ernst F. Winter from *Erasmus and Luther: Dialogue on Free Will*, New York, 1961.

Mackie, J., 1955, 'Evil and Omnipotence', *Mind*, 210.

Migne, J., n.d., *Patrologia Latina*, vols. 145 and 178, Paris.

Mill, J. S., 1887, *Three Essays on Religion*, London.

Milton, J., 1933, *De Doctrina Christiana*, New Haven.

Molina, L., 1953, *Liberi Arbitrii cum Gratiae Donis . . . Concordia*, ed. G. Rabenek, Madrid.

——, 1935, 'De Scientia Dei', in Stegmüller, W., *Geschichte des Molinismus*, Münster.

More, T., 1931, *Dialogue against Tyndale*, ed. N. Campbell, London.

Morgenbesser, S. and Walsh, J., 1962, *Free Will*, Englewood Cliffs.

Ockham, W., 1945, *Tractatus de Praedestinatione et de Praescientia Dei et de Futuris Contingentibus*, ed. P. Boehner, St. Bonaventure, New York; trans. as, 1969, *Predestination, God's Foreknowledge and Future Contingents*, ed. R. M. Adams and N. Kretzmann, New York.

Pease, W., 1955, *Cicero's De Natura Deorum*, Cambridge.

Pike, N., 1970, *God and Timelessness*, London.

Plantinga, A., 1967, *God and Other Minds*, Ithaca.

——, 1974a, *God, Freedom and Evil*, New York.

——, 1974b, *The Nature of Necessity*, Oxford.

——, 1976, 'Possible Worlds', *The Listener*.

Prior, A. N., 1957, *Time and Modality*, Oxford.

——, 1962, 'The Formalities of Omniscience', *Philosophy*.

——, 1967, *Past, Present and Future*, Oxford.

——, 1968, *Papers on Time and Tense*, Oxford.

Quine, W. V., 1953, *From A Logical Point of View*, Cambridge.

Robson, J. A., 1961, *Wyclif and the Oxford Schools*, Cambridge.

Scotus, J. Duns, *Opera Omnia*, ed. the Scotist Commission, 1950–; cited by volume number and page.

Swinburne, R., 1977, *The Coherence of Theism*, Oxford.

Tuomela, R. (ed.), 1974, *Essays on Explanation and Understanding*, Dordrecht.

Urban, P. L., 1971, 'Was Luther a Thoroughgoing Determinist?', *Journal of Theological Studies*.

Wittgenstein, L., 1956, *Remarks on the Foundations of Mathematics*, Oxford.

INDEX

Abelard, P., 9, 110–15
actualization, strong v. weak, 69
Adam and Eve, 63, 68, 81
Adams, R., 61
Anscombe, G. E. M., 34, 35, 38
antecedent v. consequent will of God, 19
a priori v. *a posteriori*, 27
Aquinas, T., 3, 7, 9, 17, 19, 25, 27, 29, 34, 38, 42, 43, 54, 91, 100–2, 110, 113, 124
Aristotle, 7, 31–2, 52
Arminius, 7, 78–9
Augustine, 15–17, 20, 25, 34, 64, 91
axioms and theorems, 27

Banez, D., 64, 75
being, 92–3
beliefs, divine, 56
Berengar, 9
Berkeley, 19–30
Bernard, 113
best possible world, 114–15
blindness, 30–1
body and mind, 123–4
Boethius, 7, 38, 106, 109
book of history, 108
Bramhall, T., 84

Calvin, J., 78–9, 86
Castaneda, H-N., 42, 46
change, real v. apparent, 41
chess, 58–9
Chisholm, R., 107
Chomsky, N., 33
clear and distinct perception, 76
compulsion, 73
computers, 123
conceivability, 122
Constance, Council of, 9
constructivism, 22–5
contingency, 52, 72, 82, 102
counterfactuals, 62–71
creation, 20

Damiani, P., 9, 100–2
Danto, A., 126

Descartes, R., 9, 16–22, 24, 27, 28, 29, 48, 76, 92
destiny, 75
determination (necessitation v. settling), 76, 85–6
determinism, 51ff.
Dort, Synod of, 79
duellists, 77
Dummett, M., 22–4, 103–9
duration, 38

Edwards, J., 82–6, 110
Erasmus, D., 72
essence and form, 21
essence of God, 17–18
essence v. existence, 9–10, 34
eternity, 54
experience, 27ff.

faith, 3, 127–9
fatalism, 52
Flew, A., 3, 64
foreknowledge, 51ff.
free to do v. free to will, 84
Freewill Defence, 66–7, 87
Frege, G., 23
future contingents, 38ff.

Geach, P., 28, 41, 45, 51, 53, 58–9, 96, 103, 124
Gibieuf, P., 75

Hilary, 63
Hobbes, T., 79–84
Homer, 6
Hopkins, G. M., 103
Hume, D., 3, 107
hypothetico-deductive method, 28

ideas, 16, 29, 30
immateriality, 124
immutability, 40–51
indeterminism, 51ff.
indifference, liberty of, 61, 83, 112

inertia, 21
inference, 25
infinite regress, 84
infinity, 93
information, 31, 44, 123
innate knowledge, 33
intuitionism, 25

Jerome, 6, 99
Jesuits, 7
Judas, 65, 74

Keilah, 63
Kenny, A., 56, 58, 85, 93
Kierkegaard, S., 127
knowledge of essences v. of reality, 19
— free v. natural v. middle, 62
— speculative v. practical, 34–6
— of understanding v. of vision, 33–4
Kretzmann, N., 40–2, 47–8

Leibniz, G., 9, 115
Lemmon, E., 44
Leo X, 72
Lewis, D., 66
logical positivism, 4
lion hunt, 104
Lucas, J., 60
Lucretius, 8
Luther, M., 60, 70–4

Mackie, J., 94
mathematics, 15–26
meaningless, 4–5
Meinong, A., 21, 23
Melanchthon, P., 78
Mersenne, M., 16–18
middle knowledge, 62
Mill, J. S., 122
Milton, J., 79–83
mistakes in performance, 35
Molina, L., 61ff.
More, T., 74

naming, 53
natural theology, 3–4
nominalists, 42

Ockham, W., 7, 9, 58
operationalism, 33
Origen, 36

pain, 29–30
pantheism, 126
paradoxes of omnipotence, 93–8
parapsychology, 106
past, bringing about, 100ff.
Paul V, 65
Pelagians, 64
perfection, 40
Peter de Rivo, 53
Pike, N., 39–40, 56
Plantinga, A., 65–71
Plato, 6
Platonism, 16, 19, 23, 25
pleasure, 32
Pliny, 8
Pope, A., 117
possible worlds, 65, 114
possibility, 92
powers, 96–100
practical knowledge, 35
prayer, 7, 103–4
predestination, 59
predictability, 72
predicates, 23
presentiality, 54
Prior, A., 39, 45, 79
private languages, 31
propositions, 44
Prosper, 63

Quine, W., 27

realism, 24
revelation, 3, 5
right v. good, 115
Ryle, Gilbert, 84

Schopenhauer, F., 51
scientia media, 62
Scotus, D., 7, 17, 19, 56, 61
sea-battle, 52, 55
Sens, Council of, 113
sensations, 28–31
sentences, 5, 23, 44
simplicity, 9
sin, power to, 109–111
Sixtus V, 53
Smith, Curley, 66
Socrates, 6
Sozzini, F., 60
Spinoza, B., 9

spontaneity, 73, 112
Stalnaker, R., 66
statement, 44
Suarez, F., 39, 61
Swinburne, R., 46, 96

telekinesis, 126
tendencies, 54
time, 38–48
timelessness, 38–40, 43, 45

Trent, Council of, 75
truth-value gap, 51, 57

Urban, L., 74

Valla, L., 72
veracity, 22
verifiability, 5, 32
virginity, 100–1
voluntarism, 19, 24